The Beer Drinker's Bible

Lore, Trivia & History: Chapter & Verse

The Beer Drinker's Bible

Lore, Trivia & History: Chapter & Verse

Gregg Smith and Carrie Getty

SIRIS BOOKS

A Division of

 brewers
publications

Boulder, Colorado

Brewers Publications, Division of the Association of Brewers
PO Box 1679, Boulder, CO 80306-1679
(303) 447-0816; Fax (303) 447-2825

Printed in the United States of America
10 9 8 7 6 5 4 3 2 1

ISBN 0-937381-56-X

Project Editor: Theresa Duggan
Copy Editor: Dianne Russell
Assistant Editor: Kim Adams
Cover and Interior Designer: Vicki Hopewell
Cover and chapter introductory art by Pearl Beach

Please direct all inquiries or orders to the above address.

Library of Congress Cataloging-in-Publication Data
Smith, Gregg, 1952–
     The beer drinker's Bible / Gregg Smith and Carrie Getty.
        p.   cm.
     Includes bibliographical references and index.
     ISBN 0-937381-56-X (alk. paper)
     1. Beer—Encyclopedias. I. Getty, Carrie. II. Title.
GT2890.S55   1997
641.2'3'03—dc21
                                                                97-39739
                                                                      CIP

To the beer committee of the Mountain Brewers Beer Fest
for all their work and dedication in building one "damn-fine" beer event:
Jerry Arrington, Bruce Baumgart, John Beal, Bob Beckwith,
Pam Byington, Rich Gelok, Tom Hartwell, Ron Leana, Jay Newkirk,
Buck Rogers, Dine Smith, and Bruce Steege. Are we having fun yet?
And with special thanks to Bob Brewer of Anchor Brewing
for the research made possible through the loan of his
personal library. We'll buy the next beer, Bob.

Jeffrey, don't give up the ship!

Contents

Introduction

In the beginning . . . This all started years ago. In fact, identifying the date of the book's origin would be extremely difficult. Over the years files, reference cards, bookmarks, clippings, labels, magazines, and books piled up deeper and deeper in what was a home office. It was a little messy at times, but a refiling here and a new bookshelf there managed to contain things. Then it happened. E-mail arrived and printouts of messages and on-line searches pushed the shelves and drawers to bursting. When floorboards and rafters began groaning it was as if the house was crying for action—"Lose weight or else."

Less patience would have resulted in a trip to the dump. Instead it was a forced march of organizing, cleaning, and gleaning that produced file after alphabetical file of beer stuff. Each piece of rediscovered information brought forth a "Hey, did you know . . ." Finally, the light bulb came on—put the stuff in a book and share it.

Writing was almost as much fun as all the beers consumed during the research, which led us all over the United States and across the pond to Europe. The trek brought new adventures and a refreshed sense of enthusiasm; it also renewed old friendships and forged new ones.

Enough of all that. Let's talk about this "bible." Unlike a conventional beer book, *The Beer Drinker's Bible* attempts to neither lecture nor influence. Instead, it represents a compilation of beer-related lore and facts with purposeful emphasis on how beer and brewing influenced history and culture.

It also references other related items, and you may find that what begins as looking up something of casual interest transforms into an extended period of reading and flipping through pages. If that happens it only means one thing—you like beer! Congratulations, you join millions of others, past and present, who've traveled the road of beer appreciation. Preceding you were some of the country's and world's greatest tradesmen and statesmen, scientists and artists, dissenters and inventors, and musicians and physicians. Beer has been around for millennia. It formed civilizations, comforted kings, crowned achievements, and consoled the common man.

A word of warning: Somewhere down the road this book might resolve some barroom dispute or validate a point made over a foaming tankard. Great! Enjoy yourself, but keep it all in perspective. It's only beer.

What Do You Call a Beer Lover?

The toughest task in beer writing is figuring out what to call the legions who enjoy beer. Specifically, how does one address that broad category sometimes called, for lack of a better name, "beer lover." After all, doesn't that seem rather simplistic? The term beer lover belies the sophistication of our drink.

So what should we call ourselves? The first thing that comes to mind are the terms other hobbyists use. There's "Trekie," which people who follow the show *Star Trek* call themselves. But it doesn't seem to convert easily. Then there's "beerie." Imagine announcing this at a social gathering, "Well, actually I'm a beerie." Slowly the crowd backs away from you until you're all alone. Nope, it simply doesn't work. At best it makes you sound like a small edible fruit—not exactly the image you want to convey. Another overused hobbyist title is "enthusiast." This won't do either. It's too common.

There's also the term used to describe those who have become so totally immersed in their passion for a subject that they've left the rest of us behind—the erstwhile "buffs." Several compelling arguments urge us to drop this line. First, we don't get as embroiled over the subject as many buffs do in theirs. Most of us are happy enough to simply drink and chat about great beers. Apart from the rather pointless alliteration of "beer buff," it sounds a little to yuppie-ish, as in "buffy." Surely that would make a beer drinker quake in disgust.

We could take a lead from those absorbed in the sports world. At first blush, "fan" doesn't seem like such a bad idea. We don't collect trading cards, although we've been known to swipe an occasional cool coaster. And we do wear shirts of our favorite teams, uh, breweries. But the mental picture of a fan includes boisterous cheering and in-your-face confrontations. That really doesn't reflect the more docile condition of beer people.

On occasion we do see some other terms used. There's the parallel to the computer world—"beer geek." But beer is a social beverage, and beer drinkers are the most affable of people; thus the image of a reclusive geek hardly seems appropriate. There's also "beer weenie." But why would we stoop to adopting such a slanderous and demeaning sobriquet?

All that reviewed, it does seem that the idea with the most merit is the suffix. The wine folks use the term *oenophile*, which means lover of wine. Maybe they're onto something. But what to use as the root word for us beer folks? We could borrow from yeast, *saccharomyces*, but then people might confuse us with terminal sweet tooths.

"Beeraphile" and "brewaphile" don't quite say it either. Surely there's a way to phrase this avocation to bestow a proper amount of dignity. Thus we are faced with turning to old reliable Latin. In this instance let's use the root word for beer—*cerevisia*. With a little prodding and twisting we get "cerevisaphile."

What better word to put in the lexicon (or argot) of beer. Can't you just see it in the dictionary? Cerevisaphile: (Cer-a-vehs-a-file) 1. an aficionado of beers and ales. 2. a devotee to the decoction of barley infused with hops and fermented. 3. an imbiber of beer of the highest order, bordering on devotion. 4. one who pursues the very finest in malted beverages.

Now that's more like it—dignified, impressive, and worthy of an inquiry from the uninitiated. Yeah. Cerevisaphile.

Beer and
Beer Drinking

ost likely the brewing of the first beer was an accident—some unplanned event wetted a store of barley. Unnoticed at first, it started to ferment. A rather simple, yet fortunate, mistake that captured the imagination of early men and women who soon set about repeating this accident again and again. By using gas chromatography and gamma spectroscopy, we can verify that our ancestors had knowledge of beer in prehistoric times.

In general, scholars agree the earliest form of brewing was discovered in Mesopotamia, and from that time on wherever man went, beer went, too. Beer became an important food staple in virtually all of the world's civilizations. Later, as the Romans developed European civilization, beer was brewed in their outposts. It was there, during the Holy Roman Empire, that beer was refined in the abbeys and monasteries. By the end of the Middle Ages beer was as much a part of European life as breathing.

A. B. Not to be confused with the initials of a modern brewer, this was one of the early names for a mixture of two English beers. It consisted of equal parts of mild and bitter ales.

Abbey. Generally, this name describes a beer made in the style of a Trappist beer. Abbey beers cannot be labeled Trappist, however, because although they are authorized by a monastery, the actual brewing takes place outside the monastery's grounds. See *Trappist* in this section.

Abdijbieren. Abbey beer.

Acetaldehyde. Unpleasant and inappropriate in beer, this compound forms during fermentation and has been described as creating a sensation of apples. It decreases as beer ages and during the production of ethanol.

Adam. A legendary strong beer of Dortmund, Germany, Adam was said to have possessed an extraordinary taste and level of alcohol. One story has it that on a visit to Dortmund, King Frederick William IV of Prussia heard the celebrated ale was available and requested a tankard, remarking, it was "very welcome; for it is extremely warm." He then drained the tankard in one draft. Members of the royal delegation were familiar with its reputation but didn't offer any warning, merely smiling to one another instead.

Reportedly, His Majesty slept it off for more than twenty-four hours.

Adam's ale. Not ale at all, but rather a tongue-in-cheek reference to water.

Adjuncts. Modern brewers call grains other than malt adjuncts. Added to the grain bill, they lighten both the color and taste of beer while lowering the expense of production.

Ale (old version). Of English origin, this word when used in reference to a drink signified an ale of the period (up to the thirteenth century) that was unhopped. The meaning fell from use as hops were used; with the addition of hops the name changed to "beer." It took many years for the more bitter hopped beer to win favor over the sweeter English ales.

> *He that first brewed the hop,*
> *was rewarded with a rope*
> *and his Beer*
> *far more bitter than Ale.*
>
> ("*High and Mightie Commendation of the Virtue of a Pot of Good Ale*" [1500s])

Eventually the preservative power of hops was championed, as in the words of Mortimer: "Brew in October and hop it for long keeping." As time passed, the taste of hops in beer won out over the old style of unhopped ale, and the word *beer* replaced *ale* in the language. That was not the end of ale, though: The term ale was later revived to distinguish top-fermented ales from the bottom-fermented lager beers.

Alecie. A word no longer in use, it described the madness brought on by excessive drinking of ale: "a man . . . in flat lunasie or alecie" (1548).

Alecost. An herb (costmary) that in the days before hops came into use was added to beer as a preservative. In that era brewers experimented with a wide variety of herbs, peppers, and tree bark to help stabilize and preserve beer. With all the strange additives, beer descriptions back then probably sounded like wine reviews.

Alegar. An out-of-date term that signified spoiled or soured ale.

Alehoof. The rather unappetizing name given to a type of ivy that was used in making a beer called ale-gill. This, like alecost, was used before the preservative qualities of hops were discovered. See *ale-gill* in the Beer-Based Mixed Drinks section.

Ales. An archaic term when used in reference to an event. Ales were festivals in medieval England. The word refers to any number of celebrations, events, and fairs, and usually implied copious drinking. A list of the ales celebrated includes bid-ales, bride-ales, give-ales, cuckoo-ales, help-ales, tithe-ales, leet-ales, lamb-ales, midsummer-ales, Scot-ales, and weddyn-ales.

Algorobo beer. A reputedly sacred brew made by the Chaco Indians in Paraguay during the eighteenth century. Made from the ripe beans of carob, mesquite, and other legume-bearing trees. Women were forbidden to drink *algorobo,* which leads to speculation that men may not have wanted women around in the presence of the beans' aftereffects. Typical of the worst cases of chauvinism, the men had absolutely no sense of what fun they missed by banning coed beer drinking.

Alt beer. No German style causes more misunderstanding and argument in the United States than *altbier*. Associated with the city and surrounding area of Düsseldorf, alt represents one of the few surviving German ales. *Alt* means "old" in German, a most appropriate designation, because Düsseldorf defiantly stood with tradition as the majority of German brewers embraced a new style—lager beer.

Lager, in reference to that new style, implied the use of lager yeast, which wasn't discovered until the 1840s. Before then, all brewers used one type of yeast—ale yeast. However, unlike the yeast strain of the same name, the brewing technique called "lagering" (which simply describes the storage process) reaches further into the past. Placing beer in cool storage (lagering) enhances it; the low temperatures increase its clarity and round any rough edges. This practice rendered German ales graceful and inviting. By comparison, the ales of other countries were crude and primitive.

Thus, in regions of western Germany the introduction of lager yeast brought forth a resounding "so what." Why switch? In some towns, Düsseldorf and Köln (Cologne) among them, brewers swore never to abandon ale yeast. They carried on with tradition, and to this day alt, like its southerly cousin *kölsch*, undergoes a warm fermentation followed by a period of cold aging (lagering). Thus, the two maintain a common bond, but with the exception of the hops, the two beer relatives differ.

Served in a short cylindrical glass, alt beers have a bright appearance (clarity), but the colors run well into the deeper hues associated with brown ales. Commonly, alts from the brewhouses of Düsseldorf feature an inviting cast of bronze to dark copper. Leaving nothing to chance, brewers use specialty malts to deliberately infuse the beer with a darkness that succeeds in deceiving well-experienced palates. Although an alt beer undergoes thorough fermentation, which attenuates nearly all the available sugars, it doesn't seem thin. In fact, it offers the drinker an astonishingly firm mouthfeel. It acquires this, in part, from the use of Pilsener and Munich malts, but what one senses as full body should rightly be credited to the suggestive power of the rich bronze color.

More aggressively hopped than kölsch, both styles deliver pronounced hop bitterness while suppressing any hint of hop aroma or flavor. Hopping rates regularly average 28–40 IBUs (international bitterness units) and beyond. Surprisingly, despite this high hop addition, the beer remains smooth and well balanced.

Smooth? With those hops? How? Thank the cold aging (lagering), which lasts three to eight weeks. The low temperature somewhat softens the bite and almost eliminates the fruity character (from esters) so prevalent in ales. Indeed, alt presents a profile dramatically different from any other ale. On introduction, the unassuming aroma often confuses the drinker. It raises doubts about the ale designation and encourages speculation that the brewer omitted the hops. Don't be fooled. Alt's true personality bursts forth at the first sip. It welcomes you to world-class bitterness with a subtle undercurrent often described as acidic or sour. Not sharp, the sourness when detected resembles a transient spirit: Was it really there or was there merely the flirting of an ephemeral presence? No matter, the building malt and mouthfeel replace it at the center of attention. Then, once you're confident it will linger, the malt fades into a clean finish, punctuated with yet another intriguing dash of thirst-quenching sourness.

What a beer. Yet sadly, until recently few examples of alt were found in the United States. The industry has seen this error, and credible versions have begun to appear. When you find a good one, sit back and think of this beer's fine brewing tradition, then come back and help America clear the confusion surrounding alt.

Apache beer. A fermented beverage made by the Apache Indians from corn, wheat, and jimsonweed. It was outlawed by the U.S. government in 1885, in part because of the poisonous nature of the jimsonweed (a nightshade) used in its production. See *oafka* in this section.

Arboga. A famous beer of Sweden. One story tells of an invading army of Norwegians and Danes led by a warrior named Hako. His invading army, so much impressed by the quality of *arboga,* delayed their advance and loitered in the taverns that served it. Later, the debilitated army lost the battle.

Archdeacon. One of the many famous English college beers, this one was brewed at Merton College at Oxford. These beers were special brews used to commemorate days of celebration at the colleges.

Audit ale. Strong beer brewed in old England at established colleges. It was initially brewed at Trinity College in Cambridge and was a special beer consumed during the feast of the day of audit.

Bachelor ale. A customary practice in old England, this was in fact the forerunner of the celebration known as a bachelor party. A celebration thrown for a young man about to wed, at a bachelor ale all money paid in exchange for glasses of ale went toward helping the new couple start their life together.

Baiersk ol. An archaic name for the common ale of Norway.

Baiting of the bombard. Bombards were common drinking vessels in old England, and the term described heavy drinking, usually implying an excess.

Bantu beer. A beer from Zimbabwe and made from millet. It was a drink of the Bantu tribes, the same Bantu Warren Zevon wrote of in his classic ballad, "Roland the Headless Thompson Gunner." Also known as *kaffir* beer.

Barley. Derivations of the word *barley* have often been used in association with beer. Of all the grains from which alcoholic beverages have been fermented, barley has been and remains the most preferred.

The Wheat is like a rich man,
That's sleek and well to do,
The Oats are like a pack of girls,
Laughing and dancing too.
The Rye is like a miser,
That's sulky, lean and small,
But the free and bearded Barley
Is the monarch of them all.

(A. T., "In Praise of Ale" [1888])

Anthropologists theorize that it was the cultivation of barley to make beer that caused prehistoric wanderers to settle into communities. It takes barley to make a beer, and we owe a debt of gratitude to the barley farmers of the world. They truly were the first civilized people.

Barley bree. Of Scottish origin, the term referred to beer in general. That use evolved by the time of Robert Burns, who used it frequently in his poetry, to describe any manner of either beer or whisky:

We are na fou, we're no that fou,
But just a drappie in our e'e,
The cock may craw, the day may daw,
And aye we'll taste the barley bree!

In other regions of Scotland beyond Burns's Lowlands, it was a term for any beer or liquor in which something was boiled.

Barley broth. An outdated term referring to the process of infusing barley to extract its fermentable sugars. It was also commonly used to describe strong beer or ale. Eventually the definition evolved to include whiskey.

Barleycorn, John. Incorrectly assumed to refer to hard liquor, the old song "John Barleycorn" describes the entire story of making beer. It begins with farming, then moves on to the harvesting, storing, malting, kilning, mashing, brewing, and fermenting processes of beer making. Although beer and whiskey both share the steps of malting through fermentation, the song makes no mention of distilling (the step necessary to produce hard liquor).

Barley wine. If the old master Rubens was to paint a beer, barley wine would be his subject. Certainly such a match would be no accident; both portrait and beer would portray a full body, appreciated with age, and critics would never regard them lightly. Indeed, the classic canvas of barley wine presents the most sophisticated of beers.

Although the designation "barley wine" originated early in the 1900s, the style has undoubtedly been brewed for hundreds of years. In bygone days the style was referred to as strong ale, stingo, Burton ale, old ale, and Scotch ale.

> *Your best barleywine, the good liquor that*
> *our honest forefathers did use to drink of.*
>
> (Izaak Walton)

Many of the former names survive and frequently appear on labels, especially in the United Kingdom. But the earliest references were as "first sort" or a mark of several Xs branded onto the wooden aging barrels. The many designations shroud the origin of this style in mystery.

First appearing centuries ago in small house-breweries, use of the modern name barley wine can be attributed to the high alcohol content, which rivals that of wine, as well as to the practice of maturing in wood. Fermentation produces both products, but no other connection with wine exists.

Achieving a thorough fermentation presents the greatest challenge in making this style, because ale yeasts have limited tolerance for high alcohol levels: The yeast goes dormant and falls to the bottom of the fermentation vessel without completing its job. Brewers overcame this by using a combination of two methods. First, by "rousing" the yeast, a gentle stir back into solution, they coaxed additional fermentation. Coupled with rousing, they pitched fresh working yeast to finish the job. In a more modern practice the brewer might take a shortcut by a late pitching of alcohol-tolerant yeast strains such as those used in Champagne. The alcohol that results can run from a fairly low 7 percent to dizzying heights of nearly 15 percent. Higher levels are typical, and breweries bottle them accordingly. Therefore, be mindful of the small bottles: Sized between 6 and 8 ounces, they offer a potent little punch from their diminutive packaging.

With so much malt used, brewers aggressively hop barley wines to balance the inherent sweetness. Routinely, hops measure up to 100 IBUs (international bitterness units). How high is this? Consider any of the distinctively hoppy ales produced in the northwestern part of the United States that use abundant additions of Cascade hops—even the most bitter versions reach only to a range in the upper 40 IBUs. Although such high hop levels in barley wines are well justified, they result in traits that vary greatly depending upon when the product is sampled.

Younger versions do present a somewhat harsh disposition, but aged (cellared) barley wines bring forth a mellow personality, and after several years of maturity they yield a much different profile than they did in youth. Older versions (two years and more) will often be described in appropriately subtle terms. These include malty, sherrylike, estery, and complex. At times the style will exhibit a richness of deep fruitlike flavors, from cherries to plums, raisins, and prunes. Finer examples, aged in the customary wooden casks, will also present winelike notes of a viney, woody, slightly tannic nature.

A few breweries produce light-colored versions of deep golden hues, such as Goldie from Eldridge Pope and Fuller's Golden Pride. However, most barley wines range in color from amber to deep reddish browns. Make no mistake, although often dark, barley wines remain clear, bright, and handsome.

Served in a tulip-shaped glass or snifter, barley wines are unchallenged by any other beer for the role of relaxing nightcap. Consume them like a fine Scotch, cognac, or sherry, and slowly savor the strong malt and alcohol with underpinnings of subtle complexity. Barley wine makes a picture-perfect companion on a deep-winter's night.

Barm. An English name given to yeast or leaven. Frequently appearing in descriptions of old beer making, it was in some locales also used by the bread makers. At times the word was also used as a (now outdated) name for the froth appearing on a glass of beer.

Barm beer. Outdated term for wort expressed from the yeast.

Bavarski-Peavah. A Russian imitation of Bavarian-style beer.

Bede ale. Not a beer, but a feast used in old England as a fund-raiser to help failed businesses get a new start. Another of those in which money and gifts were exchanged for beer. Also known as bid ale.

Beer. The old definition referred to unhopped ale. The difference between the old style of beer and the new hopped version of ale was even illustrated in verse. In this case it was a humorous poem from the sixteenth century that pitted wine, beer (the old unhopped style), and ale (hopped) in an imaginary popularity contest in which all speak of their attributes.

> *Wine—I, Jovial wine, exhilarate the heart,*
> *Beer—March Beer is drink for a king;*
> *Ale —But Ale, bonny Ale, with spice and a toast*
> *In the morning's a dainty thing.*

Ale eventually pushed beer, as it was then known, out of existence. Sources report that the last of the unhopped ales disappeared in the 1500s. The word *beer* was later resurrected when lager yeast was introduced to differentiate between ale and the new lager beer.

Beer and skittles. A term from the 1800s denoting an agreeable easy lifestyle. Skittles was a popular bar game in medieval to neoindustrial England. The term calls to mind eating and drinking combined with play and entertainment.

Belgian lace. Not lace at all, it describes the foamy residue of a beer's head that continues to cling to the inside of the glass as the beer is consumed. Many experts consider Belgian lace a sign of a well-made beer.

Beoir-lochlonnach. Translated literally as "strong at sea" (the Celtic word for the Norse), this was a drink the Irish claimed the Danes fermented from heather bells. See *heather ale* in this section.

Berliner weisse. A member of the wheat-beer family brewed in Berlin. It has a high effervescence and a sour-tart finish.

Bes. A diminutive deity from the Sudan, Bes was non-gender specific. The ancient Egyptians adopted Bes as not only a god of beer but also the protector of women and children.

Best bitter. A higher-grade version (more alcohol) than a brewery's ordinary bitter. The highest grade is called special bitter.

Bever. Latin for "to drink," and the basis of the word *beverage*. In Rome, it was used to describe a small drink served between meals. See *russin* in this section.

Bever Days. Originating at Eton College, this was a custom that spread rapidly to other universities in England. It was a period during the school year when extra bread and beer was served to scholars and their friends during the afternoon.

Bid ale. An ale served to guests at feasts in old England. Partakers were obliged to exchange money for their beer. Usually this custom served to assist a business that had fallen on hard times. What can we learn from the past? How to combat a recession. Also known as bede ale.

Bier. The German word for beer.

Bière. The French word for beer. By law France has several official terms that describe the classification of beers within that country.

Petite bière	small beer
Bière de table	table beer
Bière bock	moderate-strength beer
Bière de luxe	strongest beer (with two subcategories)
Bière de choix	strong beer
Bière speciale	strongest beer

Bière d'abbaye. French abbey-style beer. See *abbey* and *Trappist* in this section.

Bière de couvent. From France. See *bière des pères* in this section.

Bière de garde. Name given to French country ales brewed to a high strength for storage over the summer months. In the days before refrigeration, March was the last month during which beer could be fermented (summer months were too hot). This practice was put into verse as a warning to brewers:

> *Bow-wow, dandy-fly'*
> *Brew no beer in July*

These higher-alcohol brews, and other styles brewed for use during the summer, were called "laying-down beers."

Bière de malt. Low in alcohol, this was a beer brewed specifically for nursing mothers and infants. It was produced through a light fermentation that was halted prematurely. The brewer then added malt extract for sweetness. No doubt such a product would be scorned in the United States.

Bière de Mars. In the border area of Belgium and France, this term was applied to beers that were brewed before the end of March. *Bière de garde* was one that could be classified as a *bière de Mars*. See *Mars* in this section.

Bière de moine. French term to describe an abbey beer.

Bière des pères. During the sixteenth century this was a famous monastery-brewed beer of France. Reportedly, it was made to quite a considerable strength. A weaker version was called *bière de couvent*.

Biiru. The Japanese word for beer.

Bi-kal. Ancient Sumerian beer that was full-strength and much sought after.

Bilbil. Once brewed in the ancient kingdom of Upper Egypt, this beerlike drink was made from sorghum, a type of millet. Its name is a corruption of the word *bulbul* (for nightingale), because when consumed to excess it caused men to sing.

Bi-se-ba. Light barley malt beer made in ancient Sumer.

Biti. A fermented drink of West Africa, which, like beer, uses the sugars in starch to produce alcohol, in its case from the tuber Osbeckia.

Bitter. One of the most popular beers in England, similar to pale ale. The difference is largely a matter of packaging. Generally, brewers bottled the style called pale ale, and bitter was produced for draft accounts only.

Black beer. This term was originally a synonym for spruce beer. It is used to describe any number of deep-colored beers.

Blackberry ale. Despite their recent proliferation, fruit beers were not invented by the microbrewery movement. Blackberry ale was one of the assorted fruit beers made centuries ago. Its recipe started with producing a strong wort from two bushels of malt, to which the brewer added a peck of fresh ripened blackberries. After fermentation the cask was stopped up and matured for six weeks. The beverage was then bottled and after two more weeks it was ready for consumption.

Bock beers. Associated with a specific time of year—Easter—bock beers were developed in the days before refrigeration. All agree that bock first appeared in the area of Einbeck, Germany, although many explanations exist for how it came by its name. One of the most believable holds that "bock" represents the corruption of the Einbeck name to "beck," which then became bock. The literal German translation of *bock* is "goat," which accounts for the illustrated billy goat used so freely on the labels of bock beers.

Bock beer procession from the turn of the century.

Full-bodied brews with a prevalent malty sweetness, bocks can include some chocolate undertones. A common bock is usually a dark beer. Like other styles, bocks have several subcategories, all brewed around the general traits of low hops with a flavor emphasis on malty sweetness and high alcohol content, generally in the neighborhood of 7 percent. Bocks drink clean with no fruitiness or any other flavors outside the lager family. See *helles bock*, *doppelbock*, and *eisbock* in this section.

Bottle ale. Used in several of Shakespeare's plays, as in *Henry IV* Part I, "you bottle-ale rascal." Bottles were first introduced during Shakespeare's time, so the reference may have been to expensive tastes.

Bottle-conditioned. A beer in which the carbonation is generated by adding beer with yeast directly to a bottle. A small amount of malt is then added before capping. Bottles are then aged, and as the yeast consumes the malt, it expels carbon dioxide. As the carbon dioxide, and therefore the pressure, increases, the beer becomes carbonated.

Bottled mild. An English term, somewhat outdated, synonymous with brown ale.

Bouche of Court. Also known as the Bouge of Court, this was the right guaranteed to British palace staff for a supply of meat and ale free of charge. It was part of the room and board supplied to the attendants to the courts of royalty.

Bousa. A type of Egyptian beer for the common people, brewed from millet and popular for more than three thousand years. In modern Ethiopia a version may be made from wheat. Some argue that this word is the origin of the word *booze*. Other spellings include *boza*, *bouza*, and *booza(h)*.

Braga. A Romanian beer made from millet and once common throughout the rural areas of early Europe.

Bragawd. Welsh ale of the late Middle Ages, *bragawd* was known in other areas as bragot. See *bragot* in the Beer-Based Mixed Drinks section.

Bragget Sunday. An English mid–Lenten Sunday during which bragget was consumed by happy parishioners. See *bragget* in the Beer-Based Mixed Drinks section.

Brasenose ale. Another of the many college beers once produced in England. It described the special beer brewed and consumed at Brasenose College, Oxford. One account states that it was an ale that was prepared by adding a pound of sugar to sweeten the ale, which was topped off with floating roasted apples. Ale was much preferred over other drinks, and the college's affection for ale was best expressed by one of the students in a poem.

> *Then long may here the ale-charged Tankards shine,*
> *Long may the Hop plant triumph o'er the Vine.*

Brasenose students often used poetry to declare their feelings about ale, whether brewing, drinking, buying, selling, or, sometimes, to explain their position on the possible repeal of a beer tax.

> *Yet beer, they tell us, now will be*
> *Much cheaper than before;*
> *Still, if they take the duty off,*
> *In duty we drink more.*

At Shrovetide the college butler was required to produce a barrel of nappy (strong) ale and then fete the event with a poem. Students celebrated the poems and ale equally, and the best would be honored through generations of students. College ales could have no more appropriate home than Brasenose. It acquired its name through beer, by being built on the site where King Alfred's *brasinium* (brewhouse) once stood. Over the years the college was built on the old brewing grounds, and brasinium evolved into Brasenose.

> *Such, glorious liquor of the olden time,*
> *When to be drunk with Ale was deem'd no crime . . .*
> *Linked with the poet's and the scholar's name,*
> *Mellow'd by age—but still with flavour higher,*
> *The pride of Brasenose, and the boast of Prior.*

Obviously, college students have always had a close relationship with beer.

Breakfast beer. Beer for breakfast? Yes! It was the original breakfast of champions. Consider what was thought a splendid Highland breakfast: Among the eggs, mutton, butter, and other treats the only low-fat thing was the "kilderkin of beer," as reported in 1771 by Tobias Smollett. Beer was consumed from morning to night as a health measure: The water of the period was dreadful and occasionally quite toxic.

If I but for my breakfast ask
then doth she laugh and jeer;
Perhaps give me a hard dry crust
and strong four shilling beer;

(Smollett, "Advice to Bachelors")

Beer was also supplied to children in the 1600s. A description of what two children in the nursery of the Lord and Countess of Northumberland received as breakfast included "a manchett, a quart of beer, a dish of butter, a piece of slat fish, and a dish of sprats."

Upon nothing as has so great and diligent ingenuity been brought to bear . . .
as upon the invention of substitutes for beer.

(Ambrose Bierce)

Brewster sessions. In old England, special sessions of the Justice of the Peace to consider new applications and renewals of beer-selling licenses.

Bride ale. In old England, ale sometimes brewed by the bride's mother to be dispensed at the wedding by the bride in exchange for a gift or money. Before long, enterprising publicans took to organizing the bride ales (also known as bid ales) in response to the increasing popularity of public weddings.

When they come home from the church, then beginneth excesse of
eatyng and drynking, and as much is waisted in one daye as were
sufficient for the two newe-married folkes halfe a yeare to lyve upon.

("The Christian State of Matrimony" [1543])

A thirsty guest would draw a beer from the wedding cask(s) and in return placed money in a bowl or basket. Proceeds were used by the newlyweds to establish their life together and were expected to total enough money to furnish the couple for up to half a year. Celebrating with a bride ale eventually evolved into the modern term *bridal.*

Bride-bush. A term combining the name of the old sign for a tavern (the "ale bush") with the ale provided at a wedding. Also known as a bride ale.

Bride-stake. Like the bride-bush this term combined the "ale stake," an old tavern sign, with the ale served at a wedding. It had the same meaning as a bride ale or bride-bush.

Bride-wain. A synonym for bride ale.

Broken beer. An old term for beer kept for such a long time that it turned sour.

Brown ale. Famous as a thirst-quenching beer of England, brown ales evolved from the family of beers called mild ales but present a much more full and strong profile. Hints of chocolate and some fruitiness from esters greet the nose and palate. In English versions of brown ale, the hops remain at a bittering level barely sufficient to balance the malt. American versions of brown ale increase both the malt, for extra alcohol and esters, and hops. Elevated hopping rates in the American brown ales produce noticeable hop levels in both aroma and taste. Historically, the name has been in existence for centuries, although older brown ales bear little resemblance to the modern version. In the older English style a brown ale was a special brew prepared and released each autumn to celebrate the harvest. See *October ale* and *harvest ale* in this section.

Brown water. An Australian slang term, used when ordering a beer.

Brune d'Aarschot. An offshoot of the Belgian brown beer style. Brewers use up to 40 percent wheat along with aged hops in its production.

Brussels lace. The residue from the beer's head that clings to the sides of the glass after the beer is consumed. It leaves behind white remnants of the head (foam), which some liken to the pattern of lace. Also used in the shortened term *lace*. See *Belgian lace* in this section.

Bung juice. British slang term for beer. Kegs were filled through a bung-hole, and the name was derived from that feature of the equipment.

Burton ale. When mentioned in old texts it describes any of the hoppy ales of Burton-on-Trent, a village in England.

*Nowe, verilie, there is no such good and wholesome a drynk
as ye old Burton ale. . . .*

The unique hoppy character was a result of efficient hop bitterness extraction resulting from Burton-on-Trent's very hard water. This effect was well known from the earliest introduction of hops into England, for an abbey was brewing on the village site from A.D. 1100.

*In a low mountain vale
that's refreshed by the gale,
Where the Abbey of Burton once stood,
A brewhouse delights the wanderers sight,
For, believe me, the tipple is good.*

Typical brewery of the Middle Ages.

In later times, Burton became closely associated with pale ale as a specialty of the region. It was most noted, once again, for its high hop bitterness. See *pale ale* in this section.

Burton-on-Trent. The town on the river Trent that provides the focal point for the famous hoppy ales produced in that region.

Buska. Early German word for beer.

Cakes and ale. A phrase most often encountered from the 1500s on, but Chaucer mentions it even earlier in the "Pardoner's Tale":

> *"But first," quod he, "here at this ale-stake,*
> *I will both drynke and byten on a cake."*

The reference was to the practice of wassailing, when spiced cakes were washed down with a bowl of beer. The wassailing was most celebrated on Twelfth Night, which fell on the twelfth day after Christmas and honored the three kings who followed the star to Bethlehem.

Carmi. An Egyptian palace beer brewed from ancient times for consumption by the palace's royal staff. Of higher quality than that provided to the common subjects but of lesser quality than that provided to the rulers.

Carouse. To drink deeply; also, any sort of drinking and merrymaking. As of late it has come to mean any form of carrying on.

Cassis. Syrup made from black currants, it can be found in some lambic beers. Europeans may also add this as flavoring to their beer when it serves as an aperitif.

Cerevisaphile. Beer enthusiast, lover, or fan.

Cerevisia. The Latin name for beer adopted by the Romans as they moved westward and discovered the Gauls' version of beer. The Romans originally thought of beer as a type of wine made from barley, hence an old use of the term *barley wine*. The Roman barley wine was a more generic name for beer; the alcohol strength was much lower in those beers than in the modern version of barley wine.

Cerevoise. A French word based on the Latin *cerevisia* that is now outdated. It described the old style of ale made without hops.

Cervesariis feliciter. A Roman saying that translates to "long life to the brewers."

Cervesia humulina. A hop-flavored *cerevisia*. It dates to A.D. 768 and appears in the charter of the Abbey of Saint Denis.

Cerveza. The Spanish word for beer (Latin-based, of course).

Champagne du Nord. Refers to the highly effervescent wheat beer (Berliner weisse) of Berlin. For Napoleon's troops, it was a reminder of French Champagne; thus, they named it the "Champagne of the North."

Champagne of the Spree. As with *Champagne du Nord,* the term refers to the Berliner *weisse* style of wheat beer.

Chancellor ale. A college ale that originated at Queens College, Oxford, it was a strong ale and aptly named after the chancellor of the college, who authorized its consumption on occasions of note.

Chang. In Nepal and Tibet this barley-based beerlike drink is consumed from ceremonial drinking cups.

Chaser. A word that defines the practice of taking a short form of drink followed by a long one. Originally it referred to a small glass of spirits followed by a much larger glass of beer. Gradually the word ceased being an exclusive term for beer and came to include a wide variety of beverages. Chasers eventually included soft drinks and also a liquid that in the early days was considered unsanitary—water.

Chateau collapse-o. One of the more curious English names for strong ale. With tongue firmly planted in cheek, it made fun of both its effect on the body and the French connection to wine.

Chi. A type of crude beer brewed from millet in India.

Chicha. A beerlike drink of the Americas made from fermented maize and at times flavored with fruit. Some writers have elevated this drink to a near-sanctified status. In reality it was a crude form of beer and in later times was sweetened and strengthened through the addition of molasses.

Chicha de segunda. A commercial variation of *chicha* that was brewed during the 1800s. It was made by mixing—or cutting—the premium *chicha flor* with *mita*, a mix of water, honey, and fermented sediment of chicha flor. It was of lesser quality than chicha flor and thus more of a mass-market drink.

Chicha flor. A commercial and high-grade variation of the traditional South American maize drink called *chicha*. This premium version was produced in the 1800s.

China ale. Occasional accounts have stated that China ale was nothing more than a tea. In fact, it was an ale in which both China root and coriander were tied in a linen bag and immersed in fermenting beer. Some brewers of China ale would also use flavorings of various spices, lemon peel, raisins, and sugar to impart a distinctive flavor.

Chiu. A wheat beer popular all over the world, this example originated in China sometime during the second century B.C. The name became synonymous with beer, and modern Chinese use the word for nearly any beer.

Christmas ale. Any of the spiced ales brewed for the holiday season and also called winter warmers and wassail.

Chung. A Tibetan word derived from the other Tibetan word for beer—*chang*. *Chung* is made from a native barley that grew and ripened at high altitudes.

Church ale. In medieval England this ale was brewed for sale at various church-related festivals. Often the church-ale was an orchestrated event. One old source explains how this was accomplished:

> The parishioners of Elveston and Okebrook, in Derbyshire, agree jointly to brew four ales, and every ale of one quarter of malt, betwixt this and the feast of St. John the Baptist next coming. And that every inhabitant of the said town of Okebrook shall be at the several ales. And every husband and his wife shall pay two pence, every cottager one pence; and all the inhabitants of Elveston shall have and receive all the profits and advantages coming of said ales to the use and behoof of the said church of Elveston.

The maintenance of the parish directly benefiting from the church-ales is illustrated in the lines inscribed on a church in Sygate, England.

> *God speed the plough*
> *And give us good ale enow,*
> *Be merry and glade,*
> *With good ale this walk was made.*

Sounds as though the parishioners were expected to do quite a bit of drinking as part of their church duties. Small wonder why more miracles and visions were seen in the old days.

Cider. A beverage fermented from the juice of crushed apples. In the early history of the American colonies beer was the number-one beverage, but by the nineteenth century it was unseated as

An early American cider press.

America's favorite. That honor went to another drink, which could be cheaply produced in abundance—cider.

Not only was cider a convenient way to store an apple harvest, it was considered an essential part of the colonial diet. Shipments of the beverage reached far beyond New England. It gained great popularity with the farmers, merchants, and plantation owners of the South. Great Americans and drinkers such as Adams, Hancock, and Jefferson all imbibed. In fact, John Adams was reported to have braced himself with a pint of cider as he started each new day. Then, just as beer seemed destined for second billing, an unusual development occurred, and the result was beer's advancement over its competitor. The agent of beer's victory over cider was a temperance movement.

The birth of this first American temperance crusade took place in Baltimore, Maryland. It was there that six friends, whose lives had been ravaged by habitual overindulgence, banded together and, in jest at first, took the pledge. Named the Washingtonians, the group soon developed the enthusiasm of zealots and carried their message by means of meetings, lectures, preaching, and testimonials. As things progressed, the center of support became deeply rooted, as it would in later prohibition movements, in rural areas. Farmers converted to the cause were caught up in the rapture of religious fervor. By the hundreds, they swore to have no part in the production of alcoholic beverages. With this intent they took to their orchards with sharpened axes and leveled acre upon acre of productive apple trees. It seems cider production was such a large part of the apple industry that no one could think of any other use for the crop. Sadly, New England lost not only its apple-growing industry but also many of its noteworthy local apple varieties.

The extent of the devastation is best shown in a story that took place years later. A city dweller taking a trip through New England had hired a local driver with a small coach to transport him through the more rural areas. The young man was a fan of Arthur Conan Doyle and the powers of reasoning possessed by his character Sherlock Holmes. In imitation of his hero, this gent practiced making his own deductions. As the pair traveled the countryside he correctly identified which farms were the homes of teetotalers. Asked if he had been to this region before, the traveler answered no but noted that his observations were elementary. Pastures of the nondrinkers remained dotted with the regular pattern of stumps from long-felled orchards.

Despite this setback, small groups of New Englanders maintained the family tradition of putting up part of their apple crops in cider. It is to them that we owe thanks for saving this historic drink. Thus, the reintroduction of commercial cider is a return to our past. As much as we refer to beer as the all-American drink, so we should with cider. Every now and again sit back with a glass and see both our country's history, and autumn in the Northeast, in a different light.

Clerk's ale. A church ale made to support the running of a local parish. Specifically, the proceeds benefited the clerk (parson) of the parish.

Cock ale. Popular in the 1700s, this curious brew included raisins, cloves, mace, and a rooster among its ingredients. Excerpts from various letters and essays of the period insist it was a first-rate brew in which the bird imparted a delightfully mellow flavor. One recipe dating from 1736 appeared in *Smith's Complete Housewife,* but a more detailed recipe stated

> Take a large cock and kill him, and truss him well, and put into a cask 12 gallons of Ale to which add four pounds of raisins of the sun well picked, stoned, washed and dried; slice dates, half a pound; nutmeg and mace two ounces. Infuse the dates and spices in a quart of canary twenty-four hours, then press the body of him extremely well, and put the liquor into the cask where the Ale is, with the spices and fruit, adding a few blades of mace; then put to it a pint of new Ale yeast, and let it work for a day, and in two days, you may broach it for use or, in hot weather, the second day; and if it proves too strong, you may add more plain Ale to palliate this restorative drink which contributes much to the invigorating of nature.
>
> *(John Bickerdyke [1889])*

Boston Beer resurrected a form of the recipe to brew a special release beer. This version ran hot beer, fresh from the boil, over the birds, thus cooking them, and the runoff was placed in the fermenters. Afterward, the birds were eaten.

Coirm. An archaic Irish word for beer, now seldom heard.

Cold tankard. With a base of either ale or cider, a cold tankard was a mixture designed as a refreshing summertime drink. Mix together

> the juice from the peeling of one lemon, extracted by rubbing loaf sugar on it; two lemons cut into thin slices; the rind of one lemon cut thin, a quarter of a pound of loaf sugar, and a half pint of brandy. To make the cup, put into a large jug, mix them well together, and add one quart of cold spring water. Grate a nutmeg into the jug, and one pint of white wine, and a quart of strong beer, ale, perry, or cider, sweeten the mixture to taste with capillaire or sugar, put a handful of balm and the same quantity of borage in flower into it, stalk downwards. Then put the jug containing this liquor into a tub of ice, and when it has remained there one hour it is fit for use. The balm and borage should be fresh gathered.

Cold tankard was held in special regard at Oxford University, where one student claimed it exhibited humanlike traits, which he listed them as blithe, cheerful, merry, neat, comely, and obliging. Sounds as though cold tankard was everything you could ask for in a mate.

Collar. Alternate name for the foam head on beer. Popular in Europe, it refers to the contrast between a dark beer, such as a stout, and its creamy light-colored head, a beerlike parallel to the collar on the local cleric.

College ale. In old England, a special ale associated with a particular college. These ales were used to celebrate a variety of special occasions. One of the college ales was the chancellors ale, which recognized academic achievement: When a student performed extraordinarily well, up to a pint of chancellor would be authorized for him. For a time, college ales moved across the Atlantic. Originally, Harvard allowed a student ration for ale, and once, when issuance of the same was ignored by the university's president, the students staged one of the first student protests in America. Unfortunately, the official nature of the college ale vanished in the United States and degenerated into the unofficial and unglamorous but always enjoyable "kegger."

Conditioning. The traditional way to carbonate beer, as in bottle-conditioned, cask-conditioned, and so on. A process in which the brewery initiates, or introduces, a secondary fermentation to the finished beer. The brewer seals the container, and the carbon dioxide generated dissolves into and carbonates the beer.

Contract brewed (contract beer). A beer or brand owned by one company but brewed under contract in another brewery's facility. These arrangements became common in the late 1980s, when growing microbreweries lacked either sufficient production capacity or the capital to expand their own plants. Often, regional breweries with excess capacity would lease their spare brewing time and tanks, thus keeping the brewery running and workers employed. A win-win situation for all concerned.

Coper. Also spelled cooper and not to be confused with barrel making (see the Beer Bottles, Barrels, Glasses, Vessels, and Measures section). This was another type of drinking vessel, a small ship plying the fishing grounds of the North Sea that would sell beer and other spirits to the fishermen.

Corn. A fermentable cereal grain often used as an adjunct within the brewing profession. Early American colonists discovered they could ferment corn (maize) and made beer from it during periods when barley was in short supply. In more modern times brewers added it to their grain bills as an inexpensive way to help keep the price of beer low. Adding corn (or rice) has become a common practice by major commercial American breweries.

Costmary. Known equally well as alecost, this is a European shrub that was used as a flavor and preservative in ale before hops were discovered. See *alecost* in this section.

Cotsale. The cotsale was a holidaylike gathering in Britain during the 1500 and 1600s for the purpose of engaging in sport and games. Of course the drinking of ale played a role equal to that of participating in the games.

Courni. An old (circa 100 B.C.) Irish ale.

Cowslip ale. Made with the flowers of cowslip (what we call primrose), this ale was brewed according to a recipe in which a bushel of the flowers was added to a barrel of ale. It was added after fermentation was complete (sort of a floral version of dry hopping). The flowers remained in the cask with the ale for two weeks, and the ale was then bottled, each bottle primed with a lump of sugar.

Crab cider. An old style of cider made from crab apples. It projects a sharp, tart, and biting taste.

Cream ale. An American beer style developed to take advantage of the popularity of lager beer. Originally a hybrid of lager and ale, it had lager's clarity and lively effervescence but a sweeter, creamy consistency, thus the name cream ale.

Creature. Actually not related to beer, but a veiled Irish reference to distilled spirits. Wherever the creature (pronounced cray-chur and often spelled craytur) appears, beer and ale will soon arrive.

Cru. Borrowed from the lexicon of wine, this word usually refers to a specific region. When used in brewing it may carry the same meaning, but more commonly breweries use it to indicate a beer of extraordinary quality.

Cuckoo-ale. An English ale presented in celebration of spring, when the cuckoo was first heard. (Not to be confused with an often-encountered side effect of overconsumption.)

Cuitje. A Belgian beer from the fifteenth century.

Cuvee. A French term for blending two products of the same kind. Although thought an exclusive term of the wine trade, it also applies to beers and can appear with regularity on bottles of outstanding Belgian and French beers.

Cwrwf. An ale of lesser quality brewed as a drink for the masses in Wales.

Dagger ale. One of the amusing pseudonyms devised by the British to describe strong ales. Both the namesake knife and this beer deserve respect and should be handled with caution. Reputed to have originated in the Dagger Inn, Holburn, London.

Dalla. Known also as *talla,* this is a crude form of barley-based beer common in Ethiopia. Sorghum is often added, and instead of hops the crushed leaves of the giscio (treelike shrub) flavor the beer.

Decanting. Bottle-conditioned beers often have a significant amount of sediment in the bottom of the bottle. Decanting involves a careful pouring of the beer that leaves the sediment in the bottle.

Deep sinker. Slang term in Australia for a long tall glass of beer.

Derbie ale. When pale ale from Burton-on-Trent was first brought to London it was often called Derbie ale. It earned that name because the beer was first transported to Derby, where it was transferred for the final leg of the journey to London.

Diacetyl. A compound producing a buttery flavor that should not appear in lagers. Some styles, such as extra special bitters and Scotch ales, may contain some diacetyl, but most other beers do not. When a brewer desires production of diacetyl, a lower fermentation temperature of the ale yeast enhances diacetyl's presence.

Diätbier. See *diet beer* in this section.

Diet beer. Called *Diätbier* in Germany, this brew was developed as a beer low in residual sugars and carbohydrates but not in alcohol or calories. It was brewed for those restricted by diabetes to a low-sugar diet. Thus, the name was in use well before the development of beers made for the calorie conscious.

Dinner ale. When pale ale was introduced, it marked a radical departure from the dark murkiness of earlier ales. It was refreshingly hoppy, complemented all types of cuisines, and was particularly attractive in the glassware on the dinner table. The name *dinner ale* announced the arrival of beer as a fitting, and attractive, accompaniment to food.

Distiller's beer. Also called wash beer, or wash, this does not refer to beer in the traditional sense. Distillers, in making whiskey, first prepare this unhopped beer, which they ferment and then distill to concentrate the alcohol in spirits.

DMS. An abbreviation of dimethyl sulfide, a compound that produces a cooked corn aroma that is totally inappropriate in beer. Brewers avoid it by bringing the wort to a fast rolling boil and cooling promptly between the boil and the pitching, or addition of yeast.

Doble-doble. A designation for a stronger than common beer brewed in old England. Queen Elizabeth I complained that brewers had abandoned the production of smaller beer (the *syngll*) and devoted all their efforts to making doble. She observed that they brewed "a kynde of bery strong bere calling the same doble-doble-bere which they do commenly utter and sell at a very greate and excessyve pryce." Eventually, Elizabeth issued an official proclamation that required the brewers to at least once a week brew "as much syngll as doble beare and more."

The brewers' persistence in brewing this more expensive beer, especially in times of grain shortages, led Elizabeth to establishing an Act of Common Council in 1654 that specified three types of beer and the price for each. The best was to sell at 8 shillings per barrel, the second at 6 shillings, and the smaller beer at 4 shillings.

Dolo. A millet-based beer of Africa flavored with various leaves and plants, depending upon the locality.

Doppelbock. A stronger version of bock with a confusing name, *doppelbock* is not twice as strong as a regular bock. The original doppelbock was brewed in the eighteenth century by monks of Saint Francis of Paula, from which sprang the Paulaner Brewery. In those days, in observance of the religious holiday of Lent there were mandatory periods of fasting. But since beer was not included among the items forbidden, the monks made what was a "liquid bread" to carry them physically (and

"Good Bock Beer" by Edward Manet.

spiritually) through this period. They must have been very happy fasters. In fact, the Paulaner doppelbock was named *Salvator* in homage to the Savior, and to this day it is released in Germany for the Easter season. Other doppelbocks continue this tradition by ending their names in "ator." They are typically very full-bodied with intense malty sweetness and alcohol in the taste and aroma. Color is dark amber to dark brown with low hops, leaving the entire emphasis on malt.

Dortmunder. Sometimes shortened to Dort and also known as export, this beer straddles the brewing line between hoppy Pilseners and the malty beers of Munich. Lightly golden-hued and with alcohol approaching 5 percent, Dortmunder offers drinkers not a compromise, but a finely crafted and well-balanced lager.

Dragon's milk. If there were dragons you could assume their milk would deliver a strong taste, thus the English used this term as another of the veiled names for strong ale.

Drink lean. From old English custom, it is the portion of ale put aside by the inhabitants of a manor for use by the lord of the manor or his steward.

Dry beer. Less sweet, or malty, than a standard beer, dry beers were developed to provide an extremely clean and crisp (dry) finish. Through using either a specially cultured yeast strain or adding enzymes, the brewers of dry beers achieve a more thorough fermentation than possible with conventional yeast. As a result, they convert more of the beer's normally nonfermentable sugars to alcohol with a corresponding lightened body and taste. Originating in Japan, the dry style naturally complemented Japanese and Chinese foods and gained near-instant popularity. The Germans call their traditional version *Diätbier*.

Dry stout. Irish stout brewers began with a style now known as dry stout, which supplied the foundation upon which all subcategories of stout were built. Roasted barley, along with a small amount of black patent malt, imparts the coffeelike personality nearly everyone associates with the style. But to stop there would unjustly toss stout onto the refuse pile of the uninspired. By no means should it suffer a reputation of singularity. For drinkers willing to delve beyond the obvious, stout unveils a masterful composition of the sublime. It offers the beer enthusiast an enigma wrapped in a pint and further clouded by a refined coarseness. To crack its mystery requires objectivity and a willingness to strip away myth.

In the traditional form of Irish dry stout, the color never approaches a depth close to opaque. Holding any of the classics up to a light rewards the drinker with captivating hues of deep garnet. Next, the aroma extends a clean salutation unencumbered by hops. Beneath the persistent aromatics of roast coffee, the first vestige of subtlety emerges in a combination of light fruitiness, hints of malt, and a trace of caramel, all graceful and understated.

As in the aroma, the coffee bitterness permeates the flavor and masks dry stout's true personality—one of many contradictions. It starts sweet yet finishes slightly bitter, builds a hoppy bite but yields no hop flavor, fades to a smoothness in midtaste, and then with a small burst of refreshing sour tartness abruptly concludes. Finally, with its soul bared and all secrets exposed, it surprises you once again, for dry stout can rightly lay claim to the position of king of the light beers. It packs a lean twelve calories per ounce and a restrained alcohol content measuring less than

4 percent. What could be better? Perhaps one of its four offspring: see *sweet stout, foreign stout, oatmeal stout,* and *imperial stout,* all in this section. For stout's origins see *stout* in this section.

Dunder oppe. Brewed in Belgium during the 1400s, *dunder oppe* was a member of the mild ale family of beers.

Easter ale. One of the many church ales of old England, it was brewed specially for the celebration of Easter.

Egg ale. Not to be confused with eggy ale, which was a beer mixed drink. In egg ale, the eggs were added directly to the beer immediately after the yeast. Starting with a standard ale recipe of twelve gallons, yeast was added, along with the gravy of eight pounds of beef, and twelve eggs. Then a pound of raisins, oranges, and spice were placed in a linen bag and left in the barrel until fermentation was complete. At that point the brew was augmented with two quarts of sack and matured for three weeks. A small amount of sugar was added to prime (carbonate) at bottling time.

Eisbock. Bragging rights for the highest alcohol level in the bock family goes to *eisbock.* The original ice beer, its name comes from the use of ice in its production. Brewers begin with a regular *doppelbock,* and then in a process called congelation first lower its temperature enough to freeze out part of the water (but not the alcohol, which freezes at a lower temperature than water does). Because alcohol remains a liquid as the water freezes, the brewer can easily remove the water by scooping out the ice crystals, thus concentrating and raising the alcohol level of the remaining beer. The beer that remains has a full body with increased sweetness and alcoholic warmth. Eisbocks run from amber to dark brown, and hops are added for balance, leaving the emphasis on the malt.

Elevenses. Drinks taken for nourishment during the day were common in England from the Middle Ages through the eighteenth century. Elevenses referred to a midmorning break for a glass of ale to revive flagging spirits.

Entire. One of the early names for porter. Before brewers started producing the style, a bartender would create the taste associated with porter by mixing equal portions of three different beers—the "entire" beer menu on hand. Yet another name was three threads. Finally, one tavern keeper grew weary of the constant mixing:

> *Harwood, my townsman, he invented first*
> *Porter to rival wine and quench the thirst;*
> *Porter, which spreads its fame half the world o'er,*
> *Whose reputation rises more and more.*
> *As long as porter shall preserve its fame,*
> *Let all with gratitude our parish name.*

According to most accounts, it was Ralph Harwood who first brewed porter in 1720. The location was on the east side of High Street, Shoreditch, London. See *porter* in this section.

Esters. Chemical compounds in beer produced as a by-product of fermentation. Alcohol and weak acids combine to produce aromatics regularly found in ales. Beer drinkers describe the effect as fruity.

Excise. Any tax placed upon the alcohol portion of any drink. See *withdrawals* in this section.

Export. Most closely associated with Dortmunder-style lager beer. Historically, the term was applied to any beer, wine, or spirit of superior quality suitable for export sale and shipment to a foreign country. It implied a higher level of quality.

Faro. Also known as faro lambic, a blend of lambic beers (non–fruit flavored), which the brewer sweetens with Belgian candi sugar.

Festbier. In Germany the festbiers don't represent a style; rather, as with English church ales, Easter ales, and so on, brewers produce these beers to accompany a holiday, festival, or local celebration.

Finings. Settling agents placed in beer, finings enhance and brighten the clarity by causing suspended matter to fall to the bottom. Finings do not qualify as an additive to beer because they "fall through" and do not remain in solution. The brewer draws off the beer and leaves the finings in the bottom of the vessel.

Finish. In speaking of the sensory experience of consuming a beverage, "finish" describes the feel and taste left in the mouth immediately after swallowing. Words used to describe the finish of a beer include crisp, lingering, bitter, sweet, cloying, and so on. When used in a spirit of excessive profundity (or when mocking those so engaged as foppish and frivolous), the terms used to characterize the finish stretch from one end of a thesaurus to the other. Do not be intimidated, it's only beer.

Fire brewing. When a brewery claims to "fire brew," it indicates the method used to heat the brew kettle. As opposed to an internal steam coil, a fire-brewed kettle works more like a pot on a gas stove: A flame directly contacts the bottom of the pot and supplies high heat for a vigorous boil. The high heat from fire brewing usually leads to a slight caramelization of the brewing (malt's) sugars, which imparts a deeper color to the finished beer. Before the appearance of the craftbrew industry, Stroh's was one of the last U.S. brewers to fire their kettles.

Floating ants. When speaking of the beers of ancient China, the term *floating ants* describes the bits and pieces of grain that floated at the top of those crude brews.

Foam. An uninspired word for the head or collar on a beer.

Fob. English brewers use this word as a synonym for froth.

Foot ale. A fund-raiser in support of a local person entering a new business. It was money paid into a kitty for the purpose of funding the old English version of a kegger. The excess money was used to help supply the lucky recipient with a footing in a new business.

Foreign stout. The first member of stout's extended family. As the name implies, it was brewed to ship beyond Ireland's shores. Although foreign stout retained the undiminished qualities of the original, it emphasized elements that naturally preserve beer. To that end, brewers fortified it with additional malt. That modification significantly darkened the beer; moreover, it increased the alcohol that helped stabilize it during transportation. To ensure balance, brewers matched the malt with a higher hopping rate, and it, too, extended the beer's life. However, raising the amount of malt inevitably led to a fuller body and production of fruity esters, which were subdued in dry stout but blossomed in the foreign version. Along with the esters another by-product was introduced: diacetyl, which lent a touch of butterscotch flavoring. The changes bulked up the low alcohol content of dry stout to 5 or 6 percent, and when this happened it infused the beer with a light scent of sweetness.

Four ale. Now outdated, a term used in England for mild ale.

Fraise. French for the flavoring imparted through the infusion of macerated strawberries. Not exclusively related to beer, the word means "strawberry." *Fraise* appears in some versions of Belgian lambic-style beers. See *framboise* and *kriek* in this section.

Framboise. A word most often used in conjunction with Belgian lambics. Macerated fruit is added to fermented beer as a second addition of sugar, which carbonates the beer. Any variety of fruits are used, and in the case of *framboise,* the fruit is raspberries. See *fraise* and *kriek* in this section.

Freshness date. Displayed on some but not all beers, the freshness date provides ready information on condition in regard to age.

Froth. Synonym for collar, foam, or fob on a beer, most often called the head.

Fruitlada. A beer that, similar to the ancient Belgian style of brewing lambics, the women brewers of Peru traditionally have made that is also spontaneously fermented. Further like the Belgians, they add macerated fruit, notably strawberries. *Fruitlada* is served in quart glasses, and the drinker will deliberately spill the first few drops in honor of Pauchua Mama (Mother Earth).

Fusel oils. Higher alcohols imparting unpleasant, harsh, bitter fragrance and taste akin to diesel oil or solvents. They form in beer when fermentation occurs at too warm a temperature. Higher-level alcohols impart the distinctive (and undesired) taste and aroma of *Fusels,* a German word that loosely translates to "rotgut."

Gale beer. A beer made largely by traditional methods and ingredients but flavored with a species of heather. See *heather ale* in this section.

Garland ale. Various evergreens and flowers placed upon "ale stakes" (tavern signs) during times of celebration in old England. See *ale stakes* and *bush* in the Taverns and Exalted Beer Titles section.

Gildenbier. A Belgian beer made of malt and wheat. It has approximately 25 percent more malt than standard beers.

Gill. Instead of hops, brewers once used tree bark, peppers, herbs, and spices to preserve beer. In the beer named gill, a ground ivy was used. See *alehoof* in this section.

Ginger ale. Not an alcoholic drink, ginger ale was one of the substitute drinks of Prohibition that remained a popular soft drink after repeal. Ginger provides a spiciness to the beverage.

Ginger beer. Some brewers produce ginger beer as a beverage fermented from the syrup extracted from ginger. At one time it was considered a temperance drink, but the alcohol can reach elevated levels.

Give ale. In bygone days in England this was an ale served for free, usually as the result of a legacy. Why do we allow such good traditions to die?

God is good. Also spelled goddisgood. No longer used, in medieval England the phrase "God is good" was the brewers' name for yeast. The name stemmed from ignorance. No one understood the process of fermentation or yeast's role in it, only that it was necessary for the making of beer. Laws dating as early as 1450 mention it, one stating that brewers had to supply "to any person axying berme called goddisgood, taking for as much goddisgood as shall be sufficient for the brewe of a quarter of malte a ferthing at the most." In later times yeast was known as barm or barme.

Gondale. Beer from the city of Lille, France, during the Middle Ages.

Gone by. An all too frequently heard term that describes a beer that has passed its prime.

Grave ale. Nordic in origin, this was beer served during or after a funeral. The purpose was to ward off the spirit of the deceased. But wouldn't a beer bash have the opposite effect?

Green beer. You might think this refers to the unappealing color of beer on Saint Patrick's Day. In brewers' terms it means a beer that has fermented but not completed the aging process.

Groaning ale. Ale served at a childbirth; the now the archaic word obviously was inspired by the process of labor. It was supplied to attendants and others at a childbirth. Also known as groaning beer.

Grouchevoi. A variation of the beerlike Russian drink made from rye and called *kvas*. In this version macerated pears are added in much the same way Belgians add fruit to lambics.

Ground ivy. Also known as alehoof, ground ivy was used before the introduction of hops to flavor beer. See *alehoof* and *gill* in this section.

Grout. During the 1600s to mid-1700s, brewers added grout, an infusion of malt and water, to most beers to increase body and flavor. The malt was often ground into a type of flour that was more finely ground than a brewer would mill for brewing, almost to a powder. Grout has also been described as the wort of the last running, which would imply it was the basis of small beer.

Gruit. Mixtures of herbs and spices infused in beer before hops were used in early Germany. Skilled hands worked at preparing the mixtures, and this evolved into a special occupation in early brewhouses. Church-controlled breweries dispensed all *gruit*. In an official decree of 1381, Archbishop Frederick of Cologne (Köln) directed all brewers to purchase their gruit directly from the church. Herbs used in its production included bog myrtle, sweet gale, marsh or wild rosemary, milfoil, yarrow, and others. Individual recipes varied, but the addition of the herbs was not left to chance or driven by mere taste. Each was selected for the medicinal value it imparted to the finished beer.

Gueuze. A blending of young and old Belgian lambics, which produces a result similar to kraeusening. The blend ages for up to one additional year, and the finished product exhibits traits reminiscent of Champagne—light, effervescent, and refreshing.

Hala. According to Archbishop Hamilton, who was traveling through Scotland in the year 1552, *hala* was a local name for Scotch ale. He described it as a "sweet white mist." He went on to say that it differed from beer in the omission of hops.

Harbor beer. Seems a curious name for a weak (or small) beer, but it's perfectly clear to anyone who's served in the navy. Besides, what other meaning could it have? Why would anyone want to name their beer after a harbor?

Harvest ale. Many cultures celebrate the autumn season, and a successful harvest, with a festival. Harvest ale is a general term for any beer associated with harvest celebrations.

> *Now that the Harvest is over*
> *We'll make a great noise,*
> *Our master, he says,*
> *You are welcome, brave boys;*
> *We'll broach the old beer*
> *And we'll knock along,*
> *And now we sing an old harvest song.*

(M. Mendez)

A special beer made for the autumn festival was horkey-beer, which was served at the harvest. See *horkey-beer* in this section.

Hathor. The ancient Egyptian goddess who takes the form of desirable young women, sometimes portrayed as having the head of an ox. Mythology has it that Ra (the sun god) was irritated with humans and turned the sometimes violent goddess Hathor loose on earth. Hathor completed her task a little too efficiently. Rather than lose face by recalling her, Ra turned the river of human blood she was spilling into beer. Hathor stopped to drink and enjoyed it so much she imbibed to the point of overindulgence, sparing humankind in the process and indirectly giving the world beer.

Heather ale. An ale from Scotland to which heather was added instead of hops to preserve beer. Sir David Smith described a rock carved into the shape of a trough near the town of Kutchester, and he reported that: "The old peasants have a tradition that the Romans made a beverage somewhat like beer, of the bells of heather, and that this trough was used in the process of making it." The only surviving clue to its production sits within the lines:

> Search Brockwin well out and well in,
> And barm for heather crop you'll find within.

One source claims heather ale was made from ingredients in the ratio of two-thirds heather and one-third hops. Over the years modern versions have attempted to replicate the original, but they use heather more as a flavoring than as the base for fermentation. Versions using heather as a flavoring follow the general guidance of an account that suggested heather ale had a base of honey or sugar for fermentation and was flavored with heather. One re-creation of heather ale was brewed in the mid-1990s and marketed commercially.

Heavy brewing. Followed by most brewers of American standard styles of beer, this process allows a facility to increase production to levels significantly higher than that possible through conventional brewing methods. Think of it as making a concentrated form of beer to which the brewer later adds water. Also called high gravity brewing in reference to the higher specific gravity (a measure of density) in the concentrated beer.

Heavy wet. No one can say why the English have so many pet names for strong beer. Are they trying to hide something? Heavy wet might be the most descriptive of them all.

Hefe. The German word for yeast, frequently encountered on bottles of German wheat beer labeled *hefeweizen,* which translates to "wheat beer with the yeast."

Hefeweizen. See *wheat beer* in this section.

Hega. A grain-based fermented beverage of Egypt, it was first brewed over three thousand years ago, and perhaps earlier.

Hek. This was a type of beer brewed from malt by the ancient Egyptians. In recent years Egyptian breweries introduced a modern version of this classic beer. Some believe the word, and the beer, caused or inspired what we call a hiccup. Alternate spellings include *hequ* and *hekt.*

Ancient Egyptian brewer making hek.

Helles bock. *Hell* is the German word for "light" and "bright." Helles bocks possess the same general characteristics of bock, except that the helles style has no chocolate undertaste. Full-bodied, helles bock has a predominant malty taste with the gold color found in Munich-style helles beer. Enough hops are added to balance the sweetness with no aroma. Alcohol levels are high.

Hequ. An ancient Egyptian malt beer also spelled *hek* and *hekt.* Records going back to 2000 B.C. mention *hequ.*

Herb beer. Not really a beer, but a mixture of herbs and sugars fermented into a type of flavored wine.

Hiccup. See *hek* in this section.

High noon. In the Middle Ages traders would pause for a drink at "high noon" to mark the end of an active day at the market. Contrary to the name, this occurred at about 3 P.M., when trading finished.

Hob-nob. This term originally described the practice of drinking in company. See *hob-nob* in the Taverns and Exalted Beer Titles section.

Hock-Tide. As people observed Fat Tuesday as one last chance for excess before Lent, so did they celebrate Hock-Tide after Easter. It was an opportunity to make up for lost time. Traditionally held on the second Monday and Tuesday after Lent, Tuesday was the day of the greatest festivities. The origin of the name was either from the German word for high, *hoch*, or in remembrance of Henry III's crossing with his army to France on *Ochedai*. The occasion was noted for women taking to the streets with ropes to lasso men, each one forced to pay a penalty. The money went to a general fund for a community party that was well oiled with ale. On occasion things ran amuck, as it did in 1252 when, in fun pushed to the limits, the village of Esseburne was set afire and burned to the ground.

Hogen. Outdated and no longer in use, the word *hogen* was the name of an English ale of legendary alcoholic strength. According to some sources, it was one of the popular spiced beers of its day. John Taylor wrote of it in 1653, saying that it was "a high and mighty drink called hogen-mogen-rug." In 1663 another person related how he got drunk on hogen: "Damnably drunk with ale, great hogen-mogan bloody ale." The name Hogen-Mogen was indeed mighty—it was the greatest of the Dutch general states. Also spelled hogan.

Honey. Brewing beer with honey was not the invention of the microbrew movement. The practice dates back to the discovery of beer by the brewers of ancient civilizations. A highly fermentable sugar, honey adds to both the sweetness and alcohol content of beer.

Honeymoon. When used in brewing, honey was seen to instill drinkers with an amorous side effect. Tradition held that a newlywed couple be supplied with a honey-infused beer for the first month (moon) of marriage. The idea was to encourage a quick conception (or at least attempts at the same). From this custom we get the word *honeymoon*.

Hopping beer. Parts of Europe added hops to beer from the mid-1600s on, but England stubbornly refused to adulterate her often spiced but unhopped ales. When English brewers finally embraced the use of hops they first called the brew hopping beer. Soon this was replaced by the simpler word *ale*.

Hops. The flower of a climbing vine. It acts as a natural preservative for beer and along with alcohol extends beer's shelf life. Before hops, a wide variety of spices, roots, tree bark, peppers, herbs, and other additives were used to stabilize beer. The earliest use of hops in beer dates to at least A.D. 600. It took several hundred years for full acceptance, but once entrenched, there was no uprooting hops' hold on beer.

> *The hop for his profit I thus do exalt,*
> *It strengtheneth drink and it flavoreth malt,*
> *And being well brewed, long kept it will last,*
> *And drawing abide, if ye draw not too fast.*
>
> *(Thomas Tusser)*

During the nineteenth century, in the late summer, working the hop harvest provided many of England's urban laborers with their only break from the city. This helped hops gain near mystical status.

Hop tonic. A highly hopped and sometimes high alcohol beer.

Horkey-beer. A special beer made for the harvest celebrations in England. It was as much a part of the occasion of the autumn festival as song and laughter.

> *And Farmer Cheerum went, good man,*
> *And broach'd the horkey-beer,*
> *And sich a mort of folks began*
> *To eat up our good cheer.*
>
> *(R. Bloomfield)*

When the meal was finished the horkey-beer was passed about the assembly until happiness filled the room. Horkey-beer was probably a regional name, but most harvesting parties followed a similar format and served their own special beer.

Horseradish ale. Spices, peppers, tree bark, herbs, and leaves were all added to beer in the centuries before hops' introduction. Brewers tried all of them and anything else they could think of to preserve beer, so why not try roots? Beer made with horseradish was one such attempt. The diarist Samuel Pepys recorded that he drank it as a remedy against "the stone."

Huff-cap. Known as a particularly strong beer in old England, its strength was said to set men's caps upon their heads in a bold, huffing (haughty, arrogant, easily offended) fashion. It was so strong "that it would make a cat speak. . . . these men hale at huff-cap, till they be red as cockes, and little wiser than their combs" (Harrison [1587]).

Huff's ale. A marketing trick in old England, a sign posted on a tavern wall proclaimed that no one was allowed more than one pot (glass) of Huff's ale at a sitting. It was, of course, a rule implemented to protect the patrons, but the results were, as one writer noted, quite the opposite: "The restraint makes them more eager to come in, so by this policie one may hufe it four or five times a day."

Humming. Strong English ale, so named because it would cause "a humming in your brain."

Hunger stones. Near the German town of Bingen the hunger stones sit, usually submerged, in the Rhine. During years of drought the river drops to a point where the stones rise above the surface of the water. When the stones were visible the drought was of enough severity to cause a grain shortage. The sign foretold hunger, and worse yet, it meant a shortage of beer in medieval Germany.

Iablochny. In Russia rye is fermented to make a beerlike drink called *kvas.* When flavored with macerated apples (as with Belgian lambics) it is called *iablochny.*

Ice beer. Beer made through the method that was the original technique for distilling. Produced from a traditional beer, ice beer has a concentrated level of alcohol attained by lowering its temperature to freezing. Water freezes, but alcohol does not: The brewer removes the frozen water crystals that form in the cold beer, leaving behind a beverage with a concentrated level of alcohol. The method, properly called congelation, is based on the traditional German method of making *eisbock.* The Canadian brewery Labatt's receives the credit for coupling the process with an American standard style beer in late 1992. Labatt's process involves dropping the beer's temperature to near 25 °F and holding it there for about two days. After ice crystals form, it is run through a filter. Beer subjected to this process has a higher alcohol level than standard beers and a finish with very little aftertaste. Ice brewing was the process referred to in the tale of Druids attempting to poison Saint Patrick.

Imiak. Homebrewed beer in Greenland goes by the name *imiak.*

Imperial stout. Inspired by a novel event, imperial stout was a child of necessity. Peter the Great was the first czar to travel beyond Russian borders, and his visit to Europe influenced imperial stout's design.

A famous beer drinker, Peter fell in love with the West's advanced brewing skill. Every beer he tried he proclaimed better than any found at home, and after his return, the Russian court issued a contract for English stout. That order brought a mixture of joy and trouble. The endorsement was wonderful, but how could it survive the long trip? Brewers applied a proven technique—high alcohol and hopping rates.

Boosting the amount of fermentable malt contributed more alcohol to the brew. It also lightened the color to an alluring complexion of reddish brown. Unlike its relatives, imperial stout possesses an assertive nose of bold hops. As it warms, evident alcohol emerges, further complemented by notes of fruit and malt. One taste validates everything anticipated in the aroma. The medium-full body delivers an almost candied malt base with a noticeable degree of buttery diacetyl. In some examples fruity esters contribute a plum or prune character. Under its complexity the coffee flavor remains, enhanced with a subtle wisp of cocoa.

India pale ale. Also known as IPA. By the later part of the eighteenth century the malting process was becoming more controllable, and brewers were able to make a pale ale (see *pale ale* in this section), and thirsty Britons lapped up the newcomer with abandon. Hogdson, a London brewer of that era, was famous for his pale ale, and he leads us to India pale.

In the late 1700s he was the most popular ale brewer in London. With easy access to shipping from the capital, Hogdson was in position to supply beer to homesick English colonists around the world. Of these, none felt so removed, nor thirsted more for the pleasures of English breweries, than the troops garrisoned on the subcontinent of India. Hogdson rightly believed this was a huge market waiting to be tapped, but how could beer survive the sea voyage around Africa?

Hogdson used three brewing methods to ensure his ale weathered the journey. First, he knew hops were a natural preservative. He reckoned an increased hopping rate would help in transit. Next, he took advantage of another natural preservative and brewed to exaggerated levels of alcohol. Finally, he used abundant dry hopping. He couldn't have guessed better: The measures not only ensured Hogdson's modified pale ale arrived intact, but the recipients considered it an improvement over regular pale ale.

Hogdson's modifications resulted in a variation both closely related to and distinctively different from pale ale. To differentiate it from pale, it was bestowed with the name of its destination, thus India pale ale.

Characteristics of this beer can, as with other styles, vary somewhat, but an IPA will always exhibit the alcohol and hopping that distinguished the original. Hogdson and his contemporaries designed their IPA with alcohol levels of a whopping 7.5–8 percent. Modern recipes usually attain a more modest yet still noticeable strength of 5.5–7 percent. Specialty malt additions of CaraPils and crystal contributes to the deep copper-amber color and provides an undertone of faint but perceptible caramel. Conditioning favors the mild end of the spectrum but at times might be considered quite lively when compared with other English ales. In general, a traditional IPA will possess a nose of perfumey alcohol, fruitiness, and malt, although newer versions frequently overshadow the malt with strong hops. English brewers typically use hop varieties of Goldings and Fuggles, whereas American renditions of IPA employ Northern Brewer, Cascade, and Chinook, which project notes of citric or grapefruitlike flavors.

Big enough to stand up to rich entrées and sauces, India pale ale may prove a bit overpowering for delicate cuisine and seafood. Try one with strong cheeses, casseroles, stews, barbecue, and all kinds of red meats. Some of our favorites include Liberty Ale from Anchor, Young's Special London Ale, and the old reliable, Ballantine's. Of course, India pales are exceptional alone, and though many drinkers favor them in winter, they're enjoyable year-round, and to paraphrase an old poem, "should be on everyone's tongue."

Irish ale. Distinctive subcategory of pale ale brewed in Ireland. Brewers of Irish ales use more crystal malt (caramel malt) than their English counterparts, which imparts reddish hues to the beer and increases the residual sweetness—the malty-sugar taste of nonfermentables, which remains after the beer is finished. In the manner of Scottish ales, low hopping rates also contribute to the sweet finish. See *Scottish ales* in this section.

Irish moss ale. A curious recipe from the 1500s to the 1600s, it was brewed by boiling one ounce of Irish moss, one ounce of hops, one ounce of ginger, one ounce of Spanish Juice, and one pound of sugar in ten gallons of water. After fermentation, a weak alcohol-based drink was bottled. There was little link between the name and any advantage gained by the addition of the Irish moss.

Irish stout. See *dry stout* in this section.

Jena. A German white beer from Lichtenhain in the 1400s that was brewed from wheat malt. The taste is described as ciderlike with notes similar to chamomile tea.

Jiu. Representing the generic word for beer in Chinese, *jiu* was initially a wheat-based beer developed on mainland China around 200 B.C.

Kaffir. A crude beer of the Bantu tribes of Africa, who brew it from millet, or sorghum. It is also reported to have been brewed from maize. It is similar to South African mealie beer.

Kalevala. Epic poems encompassing all that ancient civilizations knew and believed about their worlds are fairly common. Finland's version was the *Kalevala*, and the importance of beer to the early Finns is reflected in the far greater number verses devoted to beer than used to explain the creation of the earth.

Kaoliang. Back around A.D. 1000, in the Sung dynasty, *kaoliang* was the Chinese beer. It was brewed from sorghum, a grain prevalent in Szechwan Province.

Kas. Sumerian root word for beer. Because of beer's value in that culture, some authorities cite this word as the origin of *cash*. See *Ninkasi* in this section.

Kava. Polynesian beer made from roots. As with some other crude alcoholic beverages, chewing and spitting prepares the starches contained in the root for fermentation.

Kiesel. Old form of beer made in Europe and Russia from oats and rye. Not related to *kvas,* of the same region, which was made from rye and included berries and other flavorings.

Kohala. A word translated from Sanskrit, *kohala* was reputed to have been an alcoholic beverage produced from barley. Some sources credit this as the root word for the Arabic term *al kohl*, from which the English language derived the word *alcohol.*

Kölsch. In western Germany close to the Netherlands border sits a city with two names. Most of us know it as Cologne, but in German it's Köln. Even the beer appears to have a dual identity: It's an ale that drinks like a lager.

Köln's hometown beer is *kölsch,* one of the few beer styles classified as an appellation. This means the style must be produced in a specific town or region. It's common to restrict wines in this manner, but only a few beers may acquire such a designation.

Kölsch is a holdover from the old days in Germany when ale-style beers were king. But even then kölsch was a bit different. It was fermented warm, but a cold aging made it a little more clean and crisp than a regular ale. When lager became all the rage, the people of Köln stuck by their own. However, the relatively modern style of lager did have some impact on the brew.

The brewers of Köln cooperated together in a guild from the year 1396, so when they were called upon to protect themselves against the challenge of lager they responded as one. They identified the elements of the style, then required filtering and adherence to specific ingredients and initiated subtle changes that lightened the beer. As a result, their code was adopted by German law, and kölsch was awarded an appellation.

The city of Köln today supports more than twenty breweries that produce kölsch beer for its eager drinkers. The residents of Köln demand a beer specifically designed to quench a mighty thirst, and they get that in kölsch. Served in tall, narrow cylindrical glasses remarkably like those used in the States for a Tom Collins, each holds 25 centiliters. A kölsch glass allows a drinker to enjoy the beer's bright appearance and pale to dark straw color. The beer presents an initially light body but possesses a pleasant firmness of mouth. Brewers attribute this to the use of Vienna, Pilsener, Bayerisch, and caramel malts. Some also add a small amount of wheat, which further contributes both to the mouthfeel and the rich, long-lasting head. Kölsch almost makes you forget it's an ale. Despite the texture, it displays low levels of the fruitiness (esters) usually associated with ales. Credit this also to the old brewers' guild, which adopted a single strain of ale yeast for kölsch. To further present an image near that of lager, a finely balanced addition of bittering hops is used.

Sadly, few good examples of kölsch can be found in the United States, but if you're planning a trip to Germany be sure to stop by either Cologne or Köln; either way, you're bound to have an authentic kölsch.

Korma. Two different cultures used this name to describe a fermented grain-based drink. In ancient Egypt it was similar to a barley wine flavored with ginger. Celtic brewers used a similar name, but their beer was made from millet.

Kraeusen. Brewers call the process of adding freshly fermenting beer to a matured batch by this name. They make the addition as a way of naturally carbonating the beer. It is also a word that describes the thick foam layer that forms on the tops of vats of fermenting beer.

Kriek. A beer in which cherries are added to a lambic beer to induce a secondary fermentation in the bottle and thus carbonate the beer, imparting a sweet-tart cherry flavor. Beers with raspberries and peaches added in the same manner are named of *framboise* and *pêche,* respectively.

Kurunnu. Another of the many fermented drinks made from grains other than barley. Ancient Babylonian brewers based this beer on spelt, a relative of wheat.

Kvas. Of all the famous Russian drinks, kvas is most similar to beer. The word *kvas* translates as "leaven." In the ancient style, brewers soak loaves of bread in water, in this case rye bread is used. They then add sugar and yeast to start fermentation. Kvas is usually flavored with fruits. Most favored is the addition of bilberries, cherries, currants, pears, and raspberries. Other ingredients commonly found in recipes are mint, raisins, honey, and juniper. Although widely displaced by English-style ales, this once popular drink continues to be produced in some parts of northern Russia. Also spelled *kwass.*

Laborogal. Similar to white ale, laborogal was made in England in the 1600s and as recently as the early 1800s with grout, malt, hops, and spices. See *grout* and *white ale* in this section.

Lace. A variation on the term Belgian lace. See *Belgian lace* in this section.

Lager. One of beer's two major classifications. Cold fermentation produces a clean, crisp beer closely associated with Germany. Styles within the family include the Pilseners, Munichs, Viennas, bocks, rauch, and others.

Did the Pilgrims come ashore at Plymouth Rock? The image is etched in our national conscience. In reality, they came ashore through the surf. Most historians agree that the myth that they stepped onto

Lager beer saloon, Berlin, 1856.

Plymouth Rock was added about one hundred years after the fact. This kind of thing happens often, stories and legends replacing fact, and sometimes it starts with an ulterior motive. This reason guides historians away from popular notions when conducting research, even with beer. So it is that beer writers often credit John Wagner of Philadelphia with producing the first American lager in 1840. This is almost universally accepted, but does it stand up?

The story goes that Wagner secured a supply of German lager yeast and started brewing. Closed case, right? Maybe not. It seems as though Wagner had a very small operation in the back of his house on Philadelphia's Saint John street, near Poplar. Production from the tiny facility was reported as similar to what a modern homebrewer can turn out. It appears the size of the brewery would have restricted any commercial application, and it would have struggled to supply Wagner's German friends.

If that was the case, where, and for what reason, did Wagner get such credit? It began much later, with an essay by Charles C. Wolf in the book *100 Years of Brewing*, a series of brewery profiles amassed in 1903. In reading that account a problem comes to light. It raises the question:

Could Wolf have produced the account as a subtle and self-serving dismissal of Wagner? In doing so, Wolf would position himself as operator of the first commercial U.S. lager brewery.

The answer sits within the untold part of the story. Charles Wolf was a sugar refiner. One of his employees, George Manger, was a friend of Wagner the lager brewer, and Manger had the good fortune to receive a supply of lager yeast from Wagner. Together, Manger and Wolf began brewing. Later, in 1844, another employee, Charles Engel, who was from Bavaria, began brewing with Wolf at the sugar refinery. This was so profitable that Wolf soon gave up the sugar business and opened a separate brewery with Engel at 352-354 Dillwyn Street. Thus, by reporting the small size of Wagner's brewery, and by showing a direct passage of the lager yeast strain to Wolf and Engel's brewery, a heavily biased Wolf could ever so subtly build a claim to the first significant commercial lager brewery in the country.

What could be wrong with Wolf's account? After all, virtually every account of American lager brewing has been based on it. That in itself illustrates the problem. All the histories written after 1902 spring from only one source—the story Wolf wrote in *100 Years of Brewing*. From a historical aspect, several problems exist with Wolf's essay. First, his writing came more than sixty years after the relevant events transpired, and stories do tend to change with age. And what about the incestuous nature of it all: his own employees, Wagner, the yeast, and his brewery. Was his story accurate? Or was he clearing a place for himself in American lager brewing history?

Wolf's history has buried implications. It hinted that Wagner's brewery was of no consequence. At the same time, Wolf constructed a tale that begs the question: Was his intent to manipulate history in order to lay claim to the first commercial lager brewery in the United States? Unfortunately, Wolf was too close to the story and had too much to gain for us to accept him as a reliable single source.

If Wagner wasn't the first commercial lager brewer (according to Wolf), was it indeed Wolf who should get credit? Apparently not, for even if Wolf's story was true, he didn't establish his brewery until 1844. In this instance we should look farther west, to Saint Louis. There in

1840, Adam Lemp constructed what would become the first truly national U.S. brewery. Upon opening he brewed only ale, but according to a variety of accounts he was producing lager by early 1842.

So was the first American lager brewer Wagner, Wolf, or Lemp? We may never know for sure, but we have indications it wasn't Wolf (despite his best efforts to convince us otherwise). A claim, but only one, could be made for Wagner's small brewery (based on Wolf's account). That leaves Lemp. So maybe, just like the Pilgrims' story, the location and legend is wrong. Now where was the Battle of Bunker Hill? Breed's Hill, you say?

Lager weisse. Most brewers produce weisse beer by traditional methods that use ale yeast. However, some breweries use lager yeast, and German breweries must use the term lager weisse for beers produced in that fashion.

Lamb ale. Beer made to celebrate the arrival of spring, so named because it was drunk during the lambing time.

Lambic. One of the few brews in the world still produced with ancient methods. In the Senne valley south of Brussels, at the end of the brew day the brewers open the windows at the top of the brewhouse to cool the boiled wort. As it cools, wild airborne yeasts of the region initiate a spontaneous fermentation. When completely fermented the beers are stored over a lengthy aging period. The resulting beer has what most describe as a sweet-tart character. See *kriek* and *framboise* in this section.

Leaven. An old term for yeast seen often in the Bible. It implies fermentation. An English term of the Middle Ages with the same meaning as *barm*.

Leet ale. A beer served during the English annual courts of records in the 1600s and dispensed at an honorary dinner.

Legs. Spoken of most commonly in regard to barley wines and old ales. Heavier-bodied beers when swirled in a glass (much like wine) leave drops that run down the inside of the glass, leaving a trail of an almost thick, even coating. Beer and wine lovers both call the effect legs. Why not? They run down the glass.

Light beer. A beer that is thoroughly fermented, with little sugar remaining unfermented. Beers in this class carry advertising that touts them as being low in calories. Some brewers water down the finished beer to achieve this. Total calories for 12 ounces usually range between 90 and 140. In Germany the term refers to the color of the beer—light as opposed to dark.

Lightstruck. Beer exposed to natural light (or ultraviolet—fluorescent—light) for an extended period of time will acquire an off-flavor and aroma called lightstruck. More commonly, people refer to it as skunky. Knowledgeable consumers will reach to the back of shelves or open cases of beer to retrieve bottles that haven't been exposed to light. See *skunky* and *sunstruck* in this section.

Liquor. As pertains to beer, the designation for water used in brewing.

London ale. This does not refer to a specific style of beer. It speaks of the quality of that city's beers. It was a well-regarded title signifying the respect in which London ale is accorded by the beer-drinking public. Soft water in London produces an easy-drinking, rounded beer. Nearby hop-growing regions furnish the other well known characteristic of London ale, but as opposed to the weighty hop bite generated by the hard water of Burton-on-Trent, London ale offers a subtle yet distinctive hop flavor. See *Burton-on-Trent* in this section.

Luda. A word for the barley-based beer made by the ancient Iranian society called Ossets. The Ossets have been credited with building the largest beer-holding vessel of the ancient world, a reservoir holding over 600 liters (more than 160 gallons).

Lüttje Lage. A German small beer usually accompanied by a second glass, of schnapps, held above the glass containing the Lüttje Lage and tilted so the two drinks mix as they enter the mouth.

Madhulika. Translations of Sanskrit identify this as an alcoholic beverage made from wheat. Was it a Mideast *hefeweizen?*

Malinovoi. A variation of *kvas,* the Russian rye-based fruit-flavored beer. In this case macerated raspberries are added, in a Russian version of a *framboise.*

Malt liquor. The only question approaching the level of "What's the meaning of life?" continues to perplex millions: How do beer and malt liquor differ? If you cut to the most common denominator you find there is no difference, unless you live in the United States, which created an artificial difference—the alcohol level. Beers generally contain 4–5 percent alcohol by volume as opposed to malt liquors, which regulations define as containing alcohol in the range of 5.6–7 percent by volume.

Malzbier. Within the beer family, *malzbier* is fermented to a low alcohol content and was originally intended as a nutritional supplement for nursing mothers and young children. Guinness served mothers equally well in the United Kingdom. Why would it be bad for U.S. mothers?

Mars. Brewed in March (the end of the brewing season) during the 1400s and 1500s, this was a low-alcohol beer. In some local areas of Belgium it was consumed heated with a sugar cube. In the beginning of the style it was spontaneously fermented and thus fits loosely in the category of lambic. In the modern era of brewing the style has been abandoned.

Mary ale. As with so many other special ales, or celebrations, this one was in honor of the feast of the Virgin Mary. During the 1500s to late 1600s, it was a beer brewed to set the celebrants in a frame of mind befitting the occasion.

Mealie beer. In South Africa this is a type of beer fermented from corn or other grains.

Menquet. An ancient Egyptian goddess of beer. See *Hathor* and *Ninkasi* in this section.

Merissa. An old brewed drink of the Sudan.

Merry-goe-down. English drinkers never tired of devising new names for strong ale: Merry-goe-down surely describes the effects of consuming high-alcohol beer. In 1637 John Taylor wrote of it, saying: "It slides down merrily. . . . most pleasing to the taste." It might have gone down merrily, but it probably had a more merry influence when it hit bottom.

Metheglin. Most people now associate metheglin with spiced mead. However, when first introduced by the Welsh, *metheglin* was the term used for "spiced drink," and as such it included beer.

Carved wooden cup used for drinking metheglin, often called a "mether" cup.

Mild ale. Dark copper in color, this is a beer originally designed for mine workers and other laborers. Generally sweet, it is brewed to low levels of alcohol as a thirst-quenching beverage. It is intended for immediate and copious consumption and to avoid the intoxicating effects of stronger beers.

Milk of amnesia. A clever modern play on words that makes light of old ale's strength and its mind-numbing effects.

Millet beer. Brewed from the small grain of that name, this is a beer once found throughout Africa. The grain was germinated, boiled, and filtered repeatedly until clear, then fermented. It was commonly flavored with various leaves, bark, and tuber roots.

Mitaca. A weak fermented maize-based drink made from the sediments of *chicha* and water and honey. See *chicha* in this section.

Moenen. A mythical Belgian creature who roams the hop-growing region. Demonlike in nature, it is blamed by hop farmers for nearly any manner of misfortune they may face with their crops.

Monastery beer. Another name, though less often used, to describe an abbey or Trappist beer. See *abbey* and *Trappist* in this section.

Morning draft. Until the end of the Middle Ages it was unusual to eat breakfast. Instead, in Britain nourishment was taken in the form of a morning draft of beer.

Morocco. A curious old strong beer of England, its recipe was rumored to have been brought back by a knight from the Crusades. For years its components were a closely guarded secret; after many years it was revealed that the secret ingredient was a generous addition of beef.

Moutwyn. Literally translated from the Dutch, the word means "malt wine."

Mum (mumm). Originating in Brunswick (Braunschweig) in the late 1400s, this beer's name may have derived from Christian Mumme, who is credited as the first to brew it. Also mentioned as the source of the name is the German word *murmeln*, "to mutter."

> *The clamorous crowd is hushed with mugs of mum,*
> *Till all, turned equal, send a general humm.*

Regardless of the name's origin the drink appears to have enjoyed a position of stature. A recipe from 1682 described the method and ingredients for producing 63 gallons:

The water must be first boiled to the consumption of a third part, then let it be brewed according to art with seven bushels of wheat-malt, one bushel of oat-malt, and one bushel of ground beans. When the mixture begins to work, the following ingredients are to be added: three pounds of the inner rind of the fir; one pound each of the tops of the fir and the birch; three handfuls of Carduus Benedictus, dried; two handfuls of flowers of Rosa solis; of burnet, betony, marjoram, avens, penny-royal, flowers of elder, and wild thyme, one handful and a half each; three ounces of bruised seeds of cardamum; and one ounce of bruised bayberries. Subsequently ten new-laid eggs, not cracked or broken, are to be put into the hogshead, which is then to be stopped close, and not tapped for two years, a sea voyage greatly improves drinking.

Tis yellow, and likewise
As bitter as gall,
And strong as six horses,
Coach and all.
As I told you 'twill make you,
As drunk as a drum;
You'd fain know the name on't,
But for that my friend, mum.

Sir Walter Scott, via Mr. Oldbuck, expressed disdain for the modern breakfasts of tea and coffee, preferring "cold roast beef and mum."

Münchener. A malty beer produced entirely within the city limits of Munich. Originally dark, a new version named helles was made with a much lighter golden hue that reached greater acceptance than the initially favored original. Both have restrained hopping rates that puts the emphasis on malt in both the nose and palate. Examples labeled "Munich-style" exhibit the same general flavor profile as Munich beers but originate outside the city. The style, pioneered by Gabriel Sedlmayr, was the inspiration for the great style of Austrian red beers known as Viennas. See *Oktoberfest* in this section.

Munich style. See *Münchener* and *Oktoberfest* in this section.

N/A beer. Brewed as a standard beer, this beverage undergoes one of any number of processes to result in low or zero alcohol content. See *near beer* in this section.

Nappy ale. Writers have often mistakenly changed this to "happy ale," but it always was nappy. In England in the 1600s nappy ale described a heady or strong ale.

> *Ale is rightly called nappy,*
> *for it well set a nap upon a man's threadbare eyes when he is sleepy.*
>
> (John Taylor)

On other occasions the term was used as an adjective for a foaming ale. Another definition (depending upon context) was "intoxication." That last meaning came, as did many in that period, as a reference to the beer's head containing much air or bubbles and little else.

Near beer. A forerunner of all the N/A styles of beer, near beer was produced in the United States in the Prohibition era. Touted as a nonalcoholic beer, some actually contained (and still do) up to 0.5 percent alcohol by weight. The first near beers were produced by boiling off the alcohol, a process that greatly, and fatally, affected the taste. To this day beer drinkers look upon near beer with disapproval. Modern N/A beers are made with a method called osmosis that, though stripping some flavor, does not alter the taste as much as boiling. However, the old saying continues to say it all: Whoever called it "near" was a poor judge of distance.

Newcastle beer. Now most closely associated with brown ale, this beer's name was originally a way of identifying the beer of the Newcastle upon Tyne region in northern England. Well loved, it was another of the many local English beers honored in song.

The horrible crew
That Hercules slew,
Were Poverty-Calumny-Trouble-and Fear;
Such a club would you borrow,
To drive away sorrow,
Apply for a jorum of Newcastle Beer.

Nidaba. Ancient Babylonian goddess of beer

Nin-Bi. Ancient Sumerian goddess of beer.

Ninkasi. The Sumerian beer goddess, Ninkasi was known as "the lady who fills the mouth." Her position as a beer goddess was established earlier than 3000 B.C., making her the first of the many goddesses that appear in early religions. Honored and immortalized in the epic Sumerian poem *Hymn to Ninkasi*, her story describes the complete method of brewing beer. The Sumerians

Followers of Ninkasi drank their beer through golden straws.

brewed and enjoyed several types of beer, and Ninkasi lent her name for the Sumerian word for beer. The Sumerians based their system of barter in part on beer. In fact, the Sumerian root word for beer, *kas*, worked its way into the English language and remains with us to this day as "cash." See *Hathor* in this section.

Ninurta. Ancient Babylonian goddess of wheat and barley, the grains essential to beer making.

Nipitatum. Also known as *nipitato*. A slang term in old England used to describe strong ales.

My father oft will tell me of a drink,
In England found and Nipitato called,
Which driveth all the sorrow from your hearts.

("The Knight of the Burning Pestle")

Nog. A name used in England to describe the strong beers of that country. In the case of nog, the word appears to have been used frequently in East Anglia, although it was not limited to that area. It also referred to a number of cocktails with eggs in the recipes, including those based on beer.

Noondrink. When noon came in medieval English markets, the brisk pace of conducting trade slowed. It left the merchants time for a break, which they filled with an ale. Prior to noondrink, the practice was called high noon, which commenced at about 3:00 P.M., when the day's trading had finished.

Noonschenche. During the 1400s in England this was a customary drink of ale taken during the workday, similar to the noondrink.

Nose. A word used to describe the aroma, bouquet, fragrance, smell of a beer.

Nottingham ale. A local brew that was regionally famous in old England. It was the subject of one of the many songs written about beer. Within the verses is noted the strong connection between the church and beer.

> *Ye bishops and deacons, priests, curates and vicars,*
> *Come taste, and you'll certainly find it is true,*
> *That Nottingham Ale is the best of all liquors*
> *And who understand the good creature like you?*

Nunchion. A meal served in old England between breakfast and dinner, the name evolved into luncheon, or lunch. It is assumed a measure of beer was served with the meal.

Nutty. A flavor description that defines the effect of oxidation in heavier and darker beers. See *oxidized* in this section.

Oafka. A beer brewed by the Apache Indians from corn, wheat, and jimsonweed. Jimsonweed is a relative of the weedlike and poisonous nightshade genus. The brew was made to ferment overnight and consume the following day. It also went by the name tiswin.

Oatmeal stout. Sweet stout's texture (see *sweet stout* in this section) captured drinkers' attention and inspired a separate formulation that included oatmeal. Inducing a silky sophistication, oatmeal stout drew immediate approval. Beyond the change in mouthfeel, it largely parallels the personality of sweet stout. It offers a full body and an intriguing mix of sugared coffee, chocolate, roast, and nutty flavors. It may also expose a teasing suggestion of caramel and faint butterscotch. It contains little hop flavor or aroma.

October (October ale or October beer). Different from Oktoberfest beer, this drink is a strong ale brewed in England during the autumn.

> *So laugh, lads, and quaff, lads,*
> *Twill make you stout and hale;*
> *Through all my days, I'll sing the praise*
> *of Brown October ale.*

> *(Reginald De Koven [1891])*

During the late 1600s and the late 1700s, October was highly valued by beer drinkers; each year's release of the new October was as anticipated in those times as bock or winter holiday releases would become in the more modern era of lager.

Oil of barley. An outdated slang term for beer.

Oke. A form of Hawaiian beer made from the ti root. See *okolehao* in this section.

Okolehao. The original brew of the ancient Hawaiian Islands, it was made by baking the root of the ti plant, which yields a heavy sugar that was then fermented into a crude form of beer.

Okole maluna. A Hawaiian toast that translates as "bottoms up."

Oktoberfest beers. Autumn brings a special celebration to Germany, a party that honors the 1810 marriage of Prince Ludwig of Bavaria to Princess Theresa. The reception they threw for their subjects was such a success that no one wanted to stop, and the party continued for sixteen days. In 1811, as the couple was contemplating how to mark their first anniversary, they could think of no better way than to repeat the merry-making of their reception. But what type of beer did they drink?

To understand the history associated with this beer, it's necessary to go back to the days before refrigeration. Although brewers at that time didn't understand why, the beers they made in the summer tended to have undesirable off-flavors and aromas. To combat this, Germany instituted a law that forbade the production of beer during the warmer months. Faced with the prospect of no production for months, brewers were forced to stockpile a beer supply large enough to meet summer's demand. The lack of refrigeration required a beer that would keep over several months. Fortunately, the best known preservative of the day was already in the beer—alcohol. Thus, brewers started producing a higher strength beer to carry them through the nonbrewing months.

The famous wedding was held at the end of the no-brewing season, so the celebration was a good excuse to knock off the stored beer while making room for new brews. This also accounts for the other name for Oktoberfest beer: *März* is the German word for "March," the last month brewing was allowed before the summer break. Ever since, Oktoberfest beer and *Märzen,* though different, have been inseparable.

Yet another Oktoberfest curiosity is the date: Most of the celebration actually takes place in September, but it varies from year to year. Here's the reason and the method to calculate when it will fall. Remember how the celebration went on for sixteen days? Well, it ended, and still does, on the first Sunday in October, thus the name. To calculate the start you only need to look up that Sunday each year and count backward sixteen days. This will allow you to amaze your friends every year, leaving only the question of what beers to serve.

Oktoberfest-style beers can vary to a certain extent, but all share some common traits. They are full-bodied, malty sweet, higher than average in alcohol, and low in apparent hops. In their modern versions the fest beers are usually, but not always, golden in color. Flavor and aroma profiles favor malt—there is very little evident hops. Brewers use just enough hops in traditional versions to balance the beer, although there may be the faintest hint of hops in the bouquet. Alcohol levels are at 4.8–5.4 percent, and in a manner of speaking these could be thought of as "baby bock" beers.

To ensure your celebration of Prince Ludwig and Princess Theresa's anniversary is as accurate as possible, stock up your fridge. We recommend Spaten, or one of the other Oktoberfest beers available from Munich.

Ol. The ancient Scandinavian word for beer. Some sources cite this as the origin of the word *ale,* which worked its way into the English language through the Saxons.

Old ale. The style of strong English ale most similar to barley wine. Very few differences exist between the two, although old ale usually appears lighter in color and is commonly found in bottled form only. See *barley wine* in this section.

Old boy. Euphemism of eighteenth century England affixed to strong ale. You can imagine its use: "Dear, I'm goin' ta town fer a while—to visit the old boy." In a sense the name was accurate—most strong ales were aged to achieve a more mellow character.

Omalofo. Possibly another name for *kaffir,* an old type of African beer fermented from millet.

Omm bilbil. Or simply *bilbil,* another of the African beers, in this case from the ancient kingdom of Upper Egypt. It was made from millet.

Ordinary bitter. The lowest in alcohol content of the three substyles of bitter. Brewed to an original gravity of 1.040 to 1.048; the next stronger is called special, or best bitter; and the strongest is called extra special bitter, or ESB. The style closely resembles the profile of a pale ale.

Osiris. Ancient Egypt worshipped numerous gods, but none was so deserving of adoration as Osiris. The god of agriculture, Osiris was honored for teaching humankind how to brew what the Egyptians called barley wine, which we know as ale.

Otibaba. Brewed in central Africa, *otibaba* is a beer made from guinea corn.

Oxidized. A term that describes a beer that has suffered the effects of oxidation. It occurs when an ale or beer has been exposed to air. Oxidation accelerates when a beer has been subjected to repeated heating and cooling. In Pilseners, lagers, and lighter ales, oxidation projects what judges describe as a wet cardboard or paper effect. In heavier ales and bocks it comes off as a nutty or sherrylike quality.

Oyster stout. Oysters in stout? Yes, oysters and stout have long been considered one of the world's great culinary combinations famous not because they taste similar—exactly the opposite. Subtle briny flavors from the oyster contrast with the roasted maltiness of Irish stout. From the late 1700s and throughout the nineteenth century, oysters and stout were found on menus of all the finest restaurants. Among commercial brewers, Colchester Brewing Company was the most well known maker of oyster stout. Beginning in 1900 it timed the annual release of its rendition to coincide with the oyster harvest. For a modern example, try McMullens.

Pachwai. A type of beer or sake made from rice in northern India.

Package. In some regions of America the phrase "getting a package on" is a euphemism for drunkenness.

Pale. The meaning of the word *pale* depends upon the context in which it is used. The speaker could use it as a reference to color, as opposed to a dark beer. It could also indicate the name of the formal and historic style known as pale ale, which in its historic context began as a way to indicate an ale of lighter color than the dark-hued beers common before pale's introduction.

Pale ale. Almost every brewpub and microbrewery lists pale ale among their beers, but why do beer drinkers get something different every place they go? How did this wide spectrum develop?

If anything, pale ale seldom appears pale. To understand the origin of the name you need to look back at the state of beer when the style originated. What ale'd England during the 1700s was an unattractive beer. Brewing was done without the benefit of temperature control in either the malting or mashing process, and the beers that resulted were, quite understandably, rather dark and murky. Acquiring the ability to kiln malt at lower temperatures and to control the degree of mashing allowed brewers to produce a beer that was much lighter in appearance. This accounts for the name, and the style was instantly popular.

So successful was the style that, in a time when beer was more important than water, it was immortalized in verse: "O' Beer! O' Hogdson, Guinness, Allsopp, Bass, names that should be on every infants tongue." We remember two of these four brands to this day, but, surprisingly, three of them were pale ales.

At the advent of the current microbrewery movement, *pale ale* was a term easily understood as a light crossover beer. Although some breweries took advantage of this term, others remained staunch traditionalists, and still others straddled the developing spectrum. Soon there was a wide range of pale ales. But what was the classic profile of this beer?

First and foremost, pale ales were characterized by a deep copper color, but Burton-on-Trent left a distinctive mark on this beer. Burton-on-Trent's water was drawn from wells in an area laden with gypsum, creating extreme hardness in the water. In the brew kettle it accounted for the most notable aspect of pale ale—aggressive hop flavor. Perhaps that's why the poet A. E. Housman penned the words "Say, or what were hop yards meant, or why was Burton built on Trent?" However, although England uses traditional English hops, American brewers substitute local varieties that gave their pale ales a citruslike flavor.

Another prominent characteristic of pale ales is a significant level of fruitiness. However, high hop levels often mask this trait in American versions. Low carbonation in the English styles of pale ale permits discerning palates to detect a slight flavor of caramel in midtaste with a low-dry maltiness and surprisingly firm mouthfeel. In some examples one can also detect low levels of diacetyl (butterscotch). Traditionally, these were bottled beers. American versions also contain these characteristics, but between the hops and a much more lively carbonation they can often prove difficult to uncover.

Although aggressive enough to stand up to heavier meals such as red meats, Italian, or Mexican food, pale ales match up equally well with richer seafoods. Sometimes a touch too bitter for salads, they do however complement a large range of cheeses. Of course they perform admirably when consumed by themselves. So the next time you pick up a pale ale think back to old England, close your eyes, and imagine the hop fields of Kent.

Panyers. Inexpensive small beer sold in the 1300s. Ale keepers charged only one-fourth as much for panyers as they did for the better, more expensive, and stronger beer.

Parsley. People once thought that the often ignored parsley was capable of preventing intoxication and drunkenness. Of course, no one in modern times would ever resort to hearsay or myth, especially before a drinking bout, in hopes of not suffering from overindulgence.

Patron saints of beer. Beer has many patron saints representing almost every facet of brewing and beer drinking. For a more complete description, see *saints* in this section.

P'ei. A crudely made Chinese beer dating to the Tang dynasty. See *floating ants* in this section.

Pennie-hweep. In regional Scottish dialect this was the word for weak ale, which in other areas of Britain was termed small beer. See *small beer* in this section.

Pepper beer. Peppers in beer have become popular in the form of chili beers. Now used for the flavor, they were originally added as a means of preserving the beer. See *spiced beer* in this section.

Perkeo. In medieval Germany, a legendary dwarf who was impervious to the effects of alcohol.

Perry. A fermented drink made with pear juice. It projects the character of the fruit and comes in versions of still, sparkling, sweet, or dry, parallel to cider. See *poire* in this section.

Petite bière. In Normandy, perhaps the most famous cider region in the world and renowned for its orchards and apples, *petite bière* is the area's old regional name for apple cider.

Peto. West African beer brewed from Guinea corn.

Pharaoh. A curious name for a strong ale, but not when it's combined with the common saying associated with it: It is so strong it will not let the people go. A strong ale was given the same name in Belgium.

Phenols. Volatile compounds that produce an undesirable flavor in beer. Related to tannins, phenols impart a plasticlike or medicinal taste to beer.

Most likely contributed by improper milling or mashing of grain, phenols also appear in beer subjected to infection or brewery cleaning compounds.

Pick-me-up. Alcohol was once thought of as a stimulant, or at least as capable of imparting a restorative effect. A drink taken for the purpose of lifting a flagging spirit or replenishing exhausted energies went by the name pick-me-up. In reality, we know that when taken to excess it works more effectively as a "lay-me-down."

Pig, drunk as a. A term thought to be derived from the drinking vessel called a piggin. A more logical explanation comes from the many similarities between human and swine anatomy, including an affinity for beer and the ability to become intoxicated. Every now and again a story surfaces of pigs that somehow get into fermented grain. Farmers report they act aggressive, grunt loudly, fight, make advances on other pigs, throw up, and sleep. Does that behavior sound oddly familiar?

Pigs ear. Cockney rhyming slang for beer.

Pils, Pilsner, or Pilsener. Style of lager beer that originated in Plzeň in Czechoslovakia. Pilseners display a yellow to light gold color in a bright, sparkling beer. Hops dominate the light maltiness, and the lager yeast, combined with cold aging, imparts a clean crisp finish of lingering hops. In some versions a light, almost imperceptible hint of diacetyl (butterscotch flavor) provides an understated complexity. When introduced, this beer offered such a dramatic alternative to the full and fruity flavor of ales that it was quickly swept into favor worldwide. The modern American brands of Budweiser, Miller, and Coors, although brewed much lighter, trace their origins to the Pilsener style of beer.

Pito. An African beer of Nigeria fermented from sorghum, a cereal grain.

Piva. A regional name for homebrew in the Aleutian Islands. It is also known as *quas* (which clearly show its Russian roots—see *kvas* in this section). The term *home-fermented* provides a more accurate description, because some examples of *piva* have very little if any grain.

Pivo. The Czechoslovakian word for beer, it has also been used as a name for beer by several American breweries. During Prohibition its reputation was corrupted when it became a brand name for near beer.

Piwo. The word for beer in Polish and in several parts of Russia.

Placbier. During the fifteenth century in Belgium this was the name for a beer of the highest quality. Beers of this type were also called *bière de luxe*.

Plough Monday. Celebrated in old England on the first Monday after Twelfth Night (see *cakes and ale* in this section), townspeople would decorate a plow and carry it from house to house, where the revelers requested bread, cheese, and ale in rather an adult version of Halloween.

Poire. French name for perry and pear, the fruity cousin of cider made by an identical process but using pears. See *perry* in this section.

Pombe. A beer brewed from millet (a small cereal grain), it was malted with the same process as for barley and then used as the base for a beer of the Guinea region in Africa. Herbs were added as much for religious and health effects as they were for flavor. In Rwanda and Uganda a beverage of the same name is brewed, but the base is prepared from the fructose-laden, highly fermentable juice of bananas.

Pombo. An African type of beer that was brewed from millet or sorghum and is related to pombe. It was a low-alcohol beer consumed during religious ceremonies. Grains were first steeped (malted) and later boiled for up to a day. After boiling, the liquid was skimmed, and the wort was fermented along with herbs to make the *pombo*.

Porter. Developed in eighteenth-century England to follow a trend in drinking, porter was a mixed beer drink comprised of equal parts of ale, beer, and two penny. Immensely popular, it had one unfortunate characteristic: It required the barkeeps to blend tankards of the stuff from three separate beer taps.

In the early 1700s the patrons of London bars were ordering a mixture called either three threads or entire. Despite common misconception, the term *three threads* did not refer to the threads on the tap (there were none), it was merely a case of vernacular speech in which "threads" equaled "thirds." The next popular name came from the tavern owner Ralph Harwood, who observed that the drink came from three separate kegs. In those days the ends (butts) of the kegs faced the patrons, and they began calling the brew a "draw of entire butt," meaning it was from all three taps.

It was only a matter of time before someone devised a means to replicate the traits of entire in one keg. Recognition as first brewer of the style

Brewhouse typical of the period when porter was first brewed.

goes to the same Ralph Harwood who called the beer entire. At the Bell Brewery in London's Shoreditch section (on the east side of High Street), during 1722 Harwood devised the style now called porter. He was credited with its invention by, among others, a Mr. Gutteridge, who put his testimonial into verse:

Harwood, my townsman, he invented first
Porter to rival wine and quench the thirst;
Porter, which spreads its fame half the world o'er,
Whose reputation rises more and more.
As long as porter shall preserve its fame,
Let all with gratitude our parish name.

The replication of entire became the rage of London. Indeed, it was immortalized in the words:

When treading London's well-known ground
If e'er I feel my spirits tire
I haul my sail, look up around,
In search of Whitbread's best entire

(*Unknown*, A Pot of Porter, Ho!)

As is evident in that admiring bit of verse, the name evolved soon after the beer's debut. It's impossible to pinpoint the first use of the term porter, but two stories are frequently cited. The first is that it was popular with the porters of London's markets. More likely it came from the second: Porters would deliver new kegs to the pubs. Their arrival would be announced with the enthusiastic call, "Porter's here!"

Regardless of the origin of the name, the new style made a huge impact on the beer world and soon jumped the Atlantic to the New World, where it became a favorite drink of George Washington. As with other beers, the popularity of porter faded and it nearly disappeared. Fortunately, the craftbrew movement and return to older styles brought back a re-creation of porter and a variety of substyles.

Typically, porter's characteristics include a dark color of deep brown with reddish garnet hues and a creamy head. The full mouthfeel is highlighted with notes of chocolate and undertones of roasty flavor. Hop bitterness is noticeable but balanced with the malt. From there the style branches into versions of English (traditional), robust, and American. English porters remain softer, malty, and more balanced. They have low hop aroma and subdued bitterness. Robust and American porters lean toward a distinct roastiness and, of course, the American rendition has prominent hopping.

Thanks to the beer revival, porters are once again popular and widely available. Match them with red meats (that's where the name porterhouse steak came from), or try them with heavier desserts. Best of all, you don't have to wait for the bartender to mix one from three different kegs—the brewery's done that for you. See *porterhouse* in the Taverns and Exalted Beer Titles section.

Potable. Drinkable, suitable for human consumption. The word is often used to describe a pleasingly drinkable liquid.

Pot ale. Not ale at all, but a rather dated term for the spent grains remaining after brewing. In a process called mashing, brewers steep grains in warm water to soak out the maltose (malt sugars) held within the barley. Later, they rinse the sugars out of the grain, producing a sweet liquor, to which they add hops and begin boiling. The grains that remain behind (the spent grains) were once called pot ale.

Potation. A word now out of use, it was once a synonym for "drinking." It was also used as a word for a draft of beer or spirits.

Premium. Used to describe the top-quality product in a brewer's line. This was a marketing term that eventually became overused, and the term *super premium* replaced it as the designation for a brewery's most expensive and high-quality brew.

Pricked beer. Alternately known as "turned beer," or beer that has gone sour. Typically this occurs after introduction of an acetic bacteria or wild yeast. Beer thus named exhibits tart and sour traits similar to vinegar.

Prima melior. A name used to classify beers, this one from circa 800 Belgium. *Prima melior* was the highest class of beer and was served on special occasions and to honored guests.

Private label. Any beer brewed under contract and displaying a brand or a brewery name that is separate from and unrelated to the production facility. Also known as contract brewing.

Profile. In reference to a style of beer, the term *style profile* or *profile* is interchangeable with the term *style description*. It provides a verbal definition of the flavor limits that make up a particular historic beer.

Prohibition. From 1920 to 1933, the "drys" forced their will on America's beer drinkers and handed them one of the bleakest periods in American history. Not only did the law of Prohibition outlaw beer drinking, it did nearly irreparable harm to the country's once proud beer culture. Its legacy has affected breweries, beer sales, and beer drinking almost seventy years after its repeal.

When did Prohibition start? How did it happen? Could beer drinkers see Prohibition again? As with any other historical issue, searching for answers leads to other and more complicated questions.

America has nearly always had a prohibition movement, its strength rising and falling and closely paralleling swings of public support for religious fundamentalism. The first American movement took place in Baltimore, Maryland, when six friends, whose lives had been ravaged by overindulgence, took the pledge. Called the Washingtonians, the group soon developed the enthusiasm of zealots and carried their message by means of meetings, lectures, preaching, and testimonials. As things progressed the center of support became deeply rooted in rural areas. Although the first attempt to pass a prohibatory law didn't succeed, the prohibitionists never gave up.

In 1919 a number of factors enabled the prohibitionists to finally carry the issue. How? First, their religious base was able to align itself with the country's Women's Suffrage movement. In addition, they waged an effective public relations campaign based on ethnic prejudice and hate. Originally there was no plan to include beer in the Prohibition laws, but the First World War changed that. Germans were universally hated in America at that time, and they were blamed for all manner of atrocities. Prohibitionists reminded Americans that most of the brewers in America were German.

Inciting resentment against Germans wasn't the only time the prohibitionists used racial hatred to their advantage. Polls taken in 1928 indicated that a vast majority of Americans wanted Prohibition to end, and one presidential candidate was running with a promise to lead the country to repeal. When Al Smith campaigned with a promise to end the noble experiment, the prohibitionists emphasized his religious affiliation (Catholic) in a successfully dirty campaign to undermine him.

After repeal the negative effects of Prohibition lived on. Hundreds of once proud breweries lay idle, never to reopen, and by the end of the Second World War scores more would join them. American beer drinkers continue to pay high taxes on their beer and to endure regulations that vary widely from state to state. Worse yet, the government-imposed three-tiered system of distribution, which was supposed to create a level playing field, has placed small breweries at a disadvantage in competing for shelf space in a country that purchases 90 percent of its beer from liquor stores and supermarkets.

Prohibition propaganda. As simplistic and manipulative as it appears today, this was the first nationally effective public relations campaign. Striking every cord of emotion possible, the prohibitionists used tools such as the Prohibition Alphabet:

> *A* stands for alcohol, king among men, who takes them to gallows or puts them in pen.
> *B* is for beer, the slop of the brewery; it lead to the judge, and right to the jury.

C is for cruelty the demon we fear, who lives in the wine, the liquors, and beer.

D is for dram, a social or not; it leads from the moderate to the old drunken sot.

E is for early, when drunkards arise to add some more flame to their blood-shot eyes.

F is for fickle, we wish you to note the defect on drinkers, for license to vote.

G is for grog shop, a hell upon earth, where men are defiled from day of their birth.

H is for health, for happiness home, but all will be blighted in the foul liquor zone.

I is a pronoun, of dignified heft; but, bloated with liquor, there isn't much left.

J is for jug, the home drinkers pet; he fights the saloons but he is still wet.

K is for kindness; but she'll never know, who lives with a drunkard, but sadness and woe.

L is for liquor, the robber of life; he's cruel to children, and mean to his wife.

M is for millions who travel the road, in coffin and shroud, by the old whiskey goad.

N is for nickel, buys one glass of booze, though the children are hungry and the wife hasn't shoes.

O is for onion; its odors are rank, but not half so bad as a walking beer tank.

P is for plaster, a mortgage, or note, that's put on the house of the old whiskey bloat.

Q is for question; is a man really sane, who drinks of a poison that injures his brain.

R is for reason; where reason should be, is absent in men who go on a spree.

S is for slicker, a saloon keepers trait; for he gets all the suckers in town on his bait.

T is for trixter, the breweryman's suit; he'll take all you have, and your own soul to boot.

U is for uncle, our dear Uncle Sam; his battle with liquor is not any sham.

V is for virtue, the greatest of all; exposed through to liquor, this virtue must fall.

W is for will power, hard liquor destroys in the great and the small, the men and the boys.

X is for quantity; of course it's unknown, but equal at least to an old whiskey drone.

Y is for youth, an age of content; but liquor indulged will make it misspent.

Z is for Zion the church of our King, who judges a nation, a misguided thing when'er it is married by the foul liquor crew, and takes the blood money of cursed revenue. But let us, by voting, the victory bring, and give to the nation a temperance ring.

Prohibition-style beer. Because commercial beers were illegal during Prohibition, many citizens began brewing beer at home. Often these beers were hastily made and of inferior quality and included substitute sugars for malt. Cheap replacements (in particular table sugar) resulted in beer with a ciderlike edge, and thereafter homebrews displaying those qualities were called Prohibition style.

Pull date (freshness date). As with other foods, beer can go stale, and breweries, in the same manner as dairies and bakeries, calculate a planned shelf life for their products. Pull dates help the distributor, retailer, and, when not hidden in code, consumer identify when a product may have reached a date beyond its prime. However, other factors, including heat, cold, and exposure to light, frequently damage a fine beer well before its time.

Purity laws. Throughout history, from ancient Sumer to medieval England and medieval Germany to colonial America, beer-drinking cultures and countries have imposed purity laws. As a form of early consumer protection these laws specified the ingredients and processes brewers were authorized to use. The most famous of these was the German beer purity law of 1516 known as the *Reinheitsgebot*.

Quaff. To quaff means to drink in a large draft. It also refers to drinking from a *quaich*, a traditional two-handled Scottish drinking bowl.

Randlermass. The German name for what the English call a shandy and the French a *panache*. A drink made by mixing beer and lemonade, it has gained popularity as a thirst quencher. From German, *randlermass* has come to be known as the cyclists beer.

Rauchbier. The German word for smoked beer. In the region of Franconia, around Bamberg, breweries make this rich-tasting beer as a local tradition. In the old days malt was dried (kilned) over a fire of alder or beech wood. The smoke of the fire permeated the grain and imparted a taste and aroma similar to that found in smoked salmon and meats. Beneath the dominating trait of smoked grain, the beer has a base with all the characteristics of the Munich style, its geographic neighbor. It has an inherent maltiness, and the hopping rate is just high enough to balance the malt with little or no hop aroma evident. Fermented as a lager, *rauchbier* should have no traces of diacetyl or fruit.

Rauscher. German sparkling cider.

Real ale. In England, the group of beer-drinking activists and purists known as CAMRA (Campaign for Real Ale) uses this phrase as a synonym for cask-conditioned beer. Beer of this type undergoes a secondary fermentation to carbonate the beer in the barrel, the process results in what has been described as a smooth and creamy texture in the beer.

Ream. Outdated as a beer-related term, the word was a provincial English term for foam or cream. It was also used as a verb to describe a beer foaming or frothing.

Red beer. Any cerevisaphile can describe the color spectrum of beer. There's light yellow, deep gold, brown, and black. All pretty normal, but lately there's red lager, which seems to have appeared out of nowhere and swept the market in the mid-1990s. What style is red beer?

Such a rapid ascent in popularity could almost have been predicted, because the reds filled a void between the micros and the big boys. But perhaps the most amazing thing about red beers is that they're not new. In fact, this is the third time they've caught the public's fancy.

As far back as ancient Sumer brewers were making red beer. Records from that period divulge not only its recipe but also its name—*kassig*. However, over the millennia it fell out of favor. Thus, by the time of brewing's great awakening in nineteenth-century Europe, it was virtually unknown. Europe in the mid-1800s brought red's second coming. In fact, it came in response to another popular style. In 1841 Munich brewer Gabriel Sedlmayr was pioneering lager brewing. Bright, golden, and malty, lager was an immediate sensation. Collaborating with Sedlmayr on this development was Austrian brewer Anton Dreher, but a number of factors prevented an exact duplication of the Munich style back in Dreher's hometown of Vienna. Both the brewing water and the available malt differed from that used by Sedlmayr. The malt in particular was unique, and it brought Dreher lasting fame.

Vienna malt was kilned (dried after malting) at a higher temperature than was the malt in Munich. As a result, the beer had two characteristics that diverged from the Munich style: It presented a toastylike flavor and an attractive reddish hue.

Despite the Vienna style's several decades of popularity, it, too, fell out of favor. Luckily, Austrian immigrants to Mexico in the later 1800s took the style with them before it disappeared entirely. South of the border the style held on and in fact became quite popular, no doubt because of the manner in which it successfully complemented the local cuisine.

Mexican brewers happily continued producing their interpretation of the Vienna style under names such as Dos Equis and Negro Modela.

A third resurgence of red beer was born of the microbrewery movement. Brewers, always looking for something a bit different, were constantly researching the old styles of beer. Naturally, the Vienna style was among those rediscovered.

Excellent with any manner of spicy foods, red beers make a refreshing year-round choice. The style greets you with a reddish amber color, and complex, malty-sweet nose, and a soft hop aroma. These traits carry over in the palate with the characteristic toasty flavor, medium body, and soft malt feel. The delicate hops are detectable in the midtaste but rapidly fade to a moderately malty finish. Fine examples of this style are produced by Rogue, Berghoff, and Legacy. You may find these and others by asking for Vienna or simply "red."

Reinheitsgebot. The famous beer purity law of Germany, which some authorities cite as the world's first consumer protection law. Setting forth standards of brewing, it prohibited the use of cheap substitutes in the manufacture of beer. Basing it upon a prior law of 1487, Wilhelm VI, Elector of Bavaria, declared in 1516 that only four ingredients could be used in the production of beer. Those were malted barley, malted wheat, hops, and water. Yeast was not included in the original law but was permitted. The main objective of the *Reinheitsgebot* was to outlaw the addition of less expensive sugars that corrupted beer and instilled a coarseness not found in the pure versions.

Rince cochon. A French term that translates literally to "pig swill." But what a way to say it.

Rug. Removed from modern vocabularies, this word in old England signified a strong ale.

Runchera. The lowest quality of commercial *chicha,* it is made with, and cheapened by, large amounts of honey and water. It was a popular drink of the working class in nineteenth-century South America.

Russ. Germans may have their purity law for brewing, but what happens when the beer is in the hands of the consumer is anybody's guess. A *Russ* takes a cue from its close relative the *randlermass*, but in this version the lemonade pairs up with wheat beer.

Russin. An old name for an ale offered between meals to revitalize the spirits. See *bever* in this section.

Rye beer. A beer made of rye. Rye beers remain generally smooth because the grain bill is based on malt, and the rye is added as an adjunct.

Sage ale. Despite misconceptions about ale making a person wise, the term *sage ale* has absolutely nothing to do with Einsteinian fermentations. One school of thought says sage ale was made as a standard ale that then underwent an infusion of sage. Others speak of sage ale as neither ale nor beer but a tealike drink made by steeping the herb.

Sahti. A Finnish barley-and-rye-based beer. Traditional brewing methods extract unbeerlike flavors by filtering hot wort through branches of juniper and straw.

Saints. In the Middle Ages the Catholic Church provided the world with brewers and acted as a center of brewing science. It's no surprise that the church has such a close connection to beer and brewing. Here are profiles of the church's major beer saints.

Saint Adrian. Often recognized as the patron of beer, the world celebrates his feast day on September 8.

Saint Arnold of Soisons. Patron of the hop pickers, he was famous for ending a plague by dipping his crucifix into a vat of beer. Those who drank from the vat were cured.

Saint Arnou (or Arnold, Arnoldus, Arnould, Arnouldus). Patron saint of brewers, he was credited with saying, "From man's sweat and God's love, beer came into the world." The story of Saint Arnou should appeal to any beer drinker. After serving as the beloved bishop to the city of Metz, in France, he retired to a monastery near Remiremont, where he passed away in A.D. 640. Townspeople of Metz never forgot their kindly mentor, and in the year after his death they received permission to inter their former bishop in his old diocese. While carrying the exhumed body to its new tomb, the procession stopped in the village of Champigneulles for refreshment and rest. As the loyal followers recovered from their exertion they sought comfort in a glass of beer. Unfortunately only one was to be found in the entire town. As it was passed about, the faithful were astonished to find that the mug never went dry. Surely that was a miracle worthy of canonization.

Saint Arnou de Oudenaarde. From Belgium, this Saint Arnou lived five centuries after his French predecessor. He was also known as Saint Arnoldus the Strong. When Flemish troops were tiring during a fierce battle, he used God's power to revive the exhausted army by creating a supply of cold beer.

Saint Bartholomew. Born on the twenty-third of August, Saint Bartholomew is the patron saint of mead drinkers, who celebrate his birthday with a feast.

Saint Brigid. A noted Irish saint, Brigid was at work in a leper colony that ran out of beer. Her solution was to use the power of the Almighty to convert the bath water to beer that eased suffering.

Saint Columbanus. A Irish missionary who became a saint, Columbanus is remembered for admonishing a group of pagans about to sacrifice a barrel of ale to an idol. Columbanus blew on the keg and destroyed both it and its contents. He then lectured that beer was used exclusively for drinking and then only after praising the Lord for his generous gift. Columbanus was quoted as having a wish to "die in the brewhouse."

Saint Florian. Savour of the city of Nürnberg (Nuremburg), Germany. The city was in danger of burning to the ground when Saint Florian managed to put the fire out with beer.

Saint Hildegard. Abbess of Rupertsberg, in Germany, Hildegard had considerable influence in the early church. She was famous for her work with herbs and is often quoted for her early writings and her practice (from the beginning of the 800s) of adding hops to the brewing process.

Saint Margaret's ale. Far from beer, this was a humorous name for water.

Saison. Famous in France and beyond, saisons are laying down beers that were once brewed in spring. Their high original gravity and correspondingly high alcohol allowed them to be stored over the summer when temperatures were too hot for brewing and fermentation. They kept through the nonbrewing months quite nicely, thereby ensuring a constant supply of beer no matter the time of year.

Saisons offer the drinker a light amber to copper-colored beer with moderately high levels of alcohol. They possess a fruity nose and palate. Low hopping rates barely balance the malt. Bottle conditioned, they contain a light layer of sediment. The nose releases the earthy character commonly found in the beers of Belgium. A slight haze may ward off some drinkers, but when it's found, this fine, smooth beer should be relished as one of the world's classics.

Sake. Can you classify sake as a beer? It's brewed from grain, it's fermented, in fact, the brewing methods closely parallel the traditional methods of making beer. Okay, we'll take it.

Sanglo. A Chinese rice beer that was brewed regularly from A.D. 600 to 900.

Schankbier. In Germany, a weak beer often prepared from the second running of the mash. Alcohol levels usually remain well below 3 percent. See *small beer* in this section.

Schenk. In Germany, beer made for prompt consumption. Also known as *schankbier* or small beer.

Scot ale. In the context of an event, Scot ale is similar to a give ale; however Scot ales were arranged by joint contribution. This was usually in the form of a voluntary levy and used in a variety of situations. (See *Scot ale* in the Taverns and Exalted Beer Titles section.) W. T. Marchant tells of one Scot ale that was arranged for holding courts:

> Thus the tenants of South Malling, in Sussex, which belonged to the Archbishop of Canterbury, were, at the keeping of a court, to entertain the lord or his bailiff with a drinking, or an ale, and the stated quotas towards the charde were, that a man should pay three pence halfpenny for himself and his wife, and a widow and a cottager three halfpence.

Also see *Scot ale* in the Taverns and Exalted Beer Titles section.

Scotch ale. The roots of and inspiration for Scotch ale date to the introduction of pale ale from Burton-on-Trent. The thrifty Scotch created a version of pale ale that avoided the use of costly hops and directly influenced the development of Scotch ale. Hop prices, driven high at the time by limited availability, discouraged brewers from large additions to the brew kettle. Thus, with hopping rates held in check, the beer presented a big, long, lingering taste of malt.

Fermentation in the country's chilly climate also lent its signature to the Scotch ale style. Cool fermentation with ale yeast often results in considerable amounts of diacetyl, a characteristic much reduced in warmer, more active fermentation. Described as a butterscotch flavor, diacetyl is exhibited in most Scotch ales as a primary flavor component. Finally, the peat burned to kiln (dry) the malted barley infuses a smokiness in the barley that runs from light and intriguing to aggressive, often stopping just short of heavy-handed. Although Scotch ales complement any season, try them as a winter warmer, a role they fill most ably.

Sediments. To be expected in bottle-conditioned beers, sediments are found in the bottom of the bottle. See *sediment* in the Beer Bottles, Barrels, Glasses, Vessels, and Measures section.

Shekar. Most well known as a biblical word for strong drink, *shekar* was one of the beerlike drinks of the ancient Hebrew world and was said to have been the beer Noah brought on the ark that was later brewed by his son Shem. Made from a mixture of fermented corn, dates, and honey, it was mentioned in the Book of Isaiah as a powerful drink. Customarily, it was provided to those about to perish. Later, the word evolved into the Hebrew word for inebriation, and some scholars say it is the root from which "cider" sprang. Also spelled *shecar, sekar, schechar.*

Shekete. A beer of Central Africa made from maize. See *mealie beer* in this section.

Shelf life. A way to monitor freshness. The beer industry uses this term to describe how long a beer can weather the aging process without damage.

Shimeyane. A South African drink fermented from ingredients of malted corn, brown bread, and brown sugar. It qualifies as a beer.

Ship's beer. A strong beer. The name was in wide use during the 1800s to describe the beer supplied to a ship's stores and crew.

Shirosake. Weak forms of sake go by the name *shirosake*. Brewers ferment it to an alcohol level kept at approximately 5 percent.

Shoto sake. Not a true sake. Producers use no grain in its fermentation; instead, they substitute the much less expensive cane sugar.

Shu. A type of beer made in China from millet, it originated in the Han dynasty over 2,100 years ago.

Sicera. A fermented beerlike drink made by the ancient Hebrews, *sicera* was mentioned in the Book of Leviticus. According to legend, the Israelites brought the knowledge of brewing a barley wine they called sicera with them on their exodus from Egypt. Known as a preventative for leprosy, it was a strong beer made from fruit, corn, honey, and grains.

Sidra. In Spain, sparkling cider is called *sidra.*

Sikaru. Dating from the Mesopotamia of six thousand years ago, *sikaru* was a beer the ancients made by soaking bread made of grain, honey, and dates in large earthen jars of water and allowing it to ferment. It was the beer of Ninkasi (see *Ninkasi* in this section), and with a few variations it was the beer of the ancient world. As this type of beer fermented it threw up a foam that dried into a crust atop the beer. Drawings and stories about royalty drinking through straws refer to this beer: The straws were used to pierce the crust and draw off liquid between it and the sediment lying on the bottom of the container.

Skunky. An appropriate description for the flavor beer picks up by sitting in sunlight or under ultraviolet (fluorescent) lights. In the United States beer drinkers use the adjective *skunky*, whereas in Europe (where they have no skunks) the term used is *catty.* Brown bottles best guard against this effect, followed by green glass. Clear bottles render virtually no protection. See *lightstruck* and *sunstruck* in this section.

Small beer. Not small in stature or size, this is rather a reference to the alcohol content of the beer. Originally this was a beer produced in England after the brewery's standard beer was extracted from a load of barley. The brewer would save the spent grain for making a separate batch of beer through one final rinsing of the used barley. Understandably, not much fermentable sugar was left. Small beer suffered with a name that implied weak body, taste, and alcohol—all of which it possessed. However, it was the beer for daily consumption. Despite its questionable standing, small beer filled a vital role in

England's public health in the seventeenth and eighteenth centuries. It kept people well by preventing them from drinking impure water.

As towns and society grew in England, people were dumping their trash and sewage into rivers and streams, fouling the water. Aside from tasting bad, such water can make people deathly sick. Small beer kept a bad situation from getting worse because it was nearly a daily dietary staple. No one understood that it was boiling the water in the brewing process that made it safe, and most likely they didn't care. Beer was an inescapable beverage at all meals.

Precious to me—it is the Dinner Bell
O blessed Bell! Thou bringest beef and beer.

(C. S. Calverly)

Though beer was the norm at all meals, including breakfast, (see *breakfast beer* in this section), people always favored strong beer over small.

Elizabeth Tudor her breakfast would make
On a pot of strong beer and a pound of beefsteak
Ere six in the morning was tolled by the chimes—
Oh, the days of Queen Bess, they were merry Old Times!

(Anonymous)

By no means was the lifestyle of Queen Elizabeth excessive or unusual— it was the norm.

By five or six he was up having his "morning"—a glass of ale....
When breakfast was served at eight o'clock he was ready for ...
mutton aided with ale.

(Henry G. Graham, The Social Life of the Scotland [1899])

All that understood, small beer was an important staple. George Washington had his own recipe for small beer. His handwritten notes may be seen, a cherished part of the collection, in the New York Public Library.

Smoked beer. In Germany the style is called *rauchbier* (smoked beer) because of the smoky flavor it gets from malt dried over a wood fire.

Soma. Brewed as far back as 1000 B.C., *soma* was said to have been the beer of ancient Persia. See *soma* in the Beer Bottles, Barrels, Glasses, Vessels, and Measures section.

Sor. The Hungarian word for beer. (And why not? Too much can make you either soar or sore, sometimes both, in that order.)

Sora. A Peruvian beerlike drink fermented from maize prior to the Conquest. It was of greater quality and higher alcohol content than the more common *chicha*. Provided to persons of high social station, it was also thought to have been made exclusively for Incan royalty.

Sorghum. A fermentable cereal grain of Old World grasses, generally related to maize, sorghum has been used to brew a number of alcohol-based beer-related beverages.

Soubya. Based on one of the fermentable cereal grains, in this case rice, *soubya* is a beerlike drink of Egypt.

Soured. Beer that has begun to turn bad after an inadvertent introduction of bacteria. See *pricked beer* in this section.

Ancient Egyptian beer bottles were filled with beers such as soubya *by an early method of syphoning.*

Sparkling. The quality of effervescence (carbonation, bubbles) released from a liquid specifically as a product of fermentation.

Spiced beers. Before the introduction of hops, which serve as a preservative in beer, a large variety of other additives were employed to extend its shelf life. Among items infused in the beer were long peppers, bog myrtle, tree bark, herbs, heather, garlic, and borage. Some worked, others didn't.

One can imagine how some of these beers must have tasted. Recipes for beers and beer drinks within this book contain numerous references to herb and spice additions.

Spruce beer. An ersatz beer, or one made when malt and hops was in short supply. Typical recipes relied heavily on molasses and sugars for fermentation and spruce buds for bittering and balance. Hard to say why it's not still a favorite.

Stale ale. In England during the sixteenth and seventeenth centuries this was the name given to ale that aged for at least a year in the barrel. More a figure of speech than a condemnation, stale ale was old ale. Somehow, the name *old ale* seems more appealing.

Starkbier. A classification of German beer. Starkbier (strong beer) has by law an alcohol content of at least 5 percent.

Steam beer. One of the true pre-Prohibition American beer styles, steam beer was born when lager's popularity was ripping through the beer world like the gold rush in California.

Aside from gold, the forty-niners' other common thirst was for the new style of beer called lager. Unfortunately, lager beer requires fermentation and aging at cold temperatures, and the environs of San Francisco provide neither—the bay has moderate conditions of about 60 °F. For brewers the obvious solution was to import ice, but the already crowded cargo ships held space at a premium, leaving no room for a cargo of such low priority. Out of desperation, brewers decided to use a lager yeast in their cool though not cold brewhouses while they crossed their fingers and hoped for the best. What they got wasn't exactly lager, but the parched mix of miners and sailors in the area didn't seem to mind. In fact, the brew soon gained popularity throughout the Pacific Coast and interior Northwest.

It was this rather warm conditioning that resulted in the pre-Prohibition steam beer name. The relatively high fermentation temperature (compared to lager) imparted a lively carbonation to the finished beer, and when a new keg was tapped it sprayed a fine mist of foam, thus earning the name steam beer.

A text dating back to the 1880s describes steam beer as a style that varied widely. As with the case of the early eastern colonists, the brewers would use whatever was available. In general the name *steam* was a vernacular expression for the brewing technique that relied upon lager yeast fermenting out the beer at warmer than usual temperatures.

The lack of adequate cooling that created the steam style beer was rectified by the late 1800s as commercial refrigeration units became commonplace and the number of steam brewers dwindled. The last surviving producer was near closing in the 1960s when Fritz Maytag decided to take a look before the brewery was gone. Little did he know he'd become the brewery's white knight. After a visit he became part owner, then owner and rebuilder in rapid succession.

Today's Anchor Steam Beer™ is built around what Maytag did and what he was able to resurrect from old brewing records. First you notice the color—a light amber, sometimes a touch cloudy but always with a high level of effervescence topped by a dense head. An aggressive hop nose is the primary aroma trait, but beyond it are hints of fruitiness, light butterscotch, and some traces of phenol/fusel (sometimes described as a light solvent taste) is a result of the warm fermentation. Taste closely follows the nose. Bitterness is achieved through copious use of Northern Brewer hops, which provide assertive yet balanced bitterness. All those hops are restrained by additions of caramel malt that along with the fruitiness and butterscotch yields a delightful balance of complexity. If that weren't enough, the carbonation dances across your tongue, stimulating your taste buds.

Steam-brewed beer. As opposed to the pre-Prohibition style known as steam beer, steam-brewed refers not to a beer but a brewing method. When breweries were first modernizing in the 1800s, the use of steam coils to heat the brew kettles was cutting-edge technology, and brewers would advertise the use of steam, some calling their brews "steam-brewed beer." An efficient mode of heat transfer, steam heating kettles remains a common choice of breweries. Thus, many breweries could say they "steam brew."

Stingo. Though now nearly outdated, this term was an early English designation for strong beer.

> *I have no Greek or Latin lingo*
> *But a fresh tap of Foaming stingo—*

By some accounts, use of stingo to signify strong beer reached its peak by the late 1800s.

> *Of hop a little quantity,*
> *And barm to it they bring too;*
> *Being barrell'd up, they call't a cup*
> *Of dainty good old stingo.*
>
> *("Merry Drollery" [1650])*

With the arrival of the twentieth century, the use of stingo largely yielded to old ale or barley wine.

Stitch. A local name from London for a strong brown ale made in the mid-1700s. It was reputed to also serve as a curative.

Stock ale. At first associated with the beer of Burton-on-Trent, stock ale was a very strong beer made with the intention of placing it in storage, in "stock," for aging.

Stone ale. Brewed in old England by the monks at Stone, Staffordshire, stone ale was a regional favorite in England. It should not be confused with the German *stein* (stone) beer, in which hot rocks bring the kettle to a boil. The Germans use this process to make a unique lager beer.

Stout. Throughout the world, crowded taverns thrill to a "shout for stout." U.S. beer drinkers might think that odd, but only until they learn why. In a vast number of Anglo-oriented pubs customers recognize "a shout" as slang for a declaration to buy the next round. It's not surprising that the grateful response usually results in a flurry of orders for stout.

First brewed in the 1700s, the stout we drink has disputed origins. Some writers describe it as the son of porter. Others insist stout existed long before. Those in this second group point to common use of the word *stout* well before porter's introduction. What they overlooked was both the form of the word and the context in which it was used. In the historical beer lexicon the word stout did precede porter, and it was used with regularity. However, prior to the late 1700s it was strictly an adjective. In the context of references dating back to the 1600s, English people were using stout to describe any type of strong ale.

When did the use of stout first signify a separate style? Stout evolved from a beer designed as a sort of superrobust porter; problem was what to call it. Here again the word stout was used as an adjective when, for lack of a better name, people referred to the new, fuller-tasting variation as a porter-stout. Eventually the name shortened and the adjective became a noun; from then on it was simply stout.

In 1759 in Ireland, Arthur Guinness closed what his peers considered a foolish real estate deal. He agreed to pay forty pounds per year for an old idle brewhouse. The unusual or foolish part was the term of the contract: nine thousand years. At first the brewery promised nothing but struggle, but his fortune changed in the 1760s when he moved away from ale. The beer he switched to was stout. Guinness brewed his with high levels of roasted grain to emphasize the coffee character. Next, he intentionally added the unthinkable—sour beer—but in a controlled amount (approximately 1 percent). He found this pleasantly dried the finish. His modifications brought rising profits and a complete switch to porter-stout in 1799 by beer drinkers. From then on stout was solidly linked to the Guinness family name.

Why did porter decline and stout triumph? It had to do with politics and war. During World War I rationing and energy restrictions in England prevented malting companies from deeply roasting grains. But Ireland, poised on the edge of rebellion and leaning toward alliance with Germany, was treated with kid gloves. No restrictions of any kind were enacted. During the war and after, England moved away from their dark beer, while Ireland continued its love affair with stout.

Other nations express astonishment that the United States waited to discover what they all knew long ago: The family of stout offers beer drinkers sophisticated taste and a great variety that pairs easily with a wide spectrum of foods. Though late to answer the call, the country's palate has finally reserved a spot for the world's favorite black beer. Proclaim your support and give a shout for stout.

Strong beer. A beer of high alcohol content. Originally, beers of this type were brewed to keep over a long period of time. Typically, the brewer was taking advantage of the preservative qualities of alcohol to make beers that would last through the warm months of the summer, when brewing was not possible.

> *He that drinks strong beer,*
> *and goes to bed mellow*
> *Lives as he ought live,*
> *and dies a hearty fellow.*

> (Fletcher's Bloody Brother)

Sucellus. Ancient Gaul's god of brewing.

Suds. A crude and uninspired synonym for beer. A beverage as noble as beer deserves more respect.

Sumerians. Of all the ancient brewers, the most knowledgeable were the Sumerians. Sumerian works on brewing date back more than five thousand years, and recipes for more than twenty different Sumerian beers survive. Using what they called *bapir*—a baked loaf of barley, grains, honey, and dates—the women brewsters of Sumer crumbled the loaves in water and allowed the mixture to ferment by means of wild air-borne yeasts. The goddess Ninkasi watched over all beer-related activities and held an esteemed position in the Sumerian religion and culture. A frequent salutation was "May Ninkasi pour your beer ever-lasting." See *Ninkasi* in this section and *Bit Sikari* in the Taverns and Exalted Beer Titles section.

Sumshu. A sorghum-based form of beer made in Manchuria.

Sundowner. This is known as the first beer of the evening in South Africa.

Sunstruck. Also known as lightstruck, this term is applied to beer that has seen exposure to the sun, which imparts a skunklike aroma or sensation. See *lightstruck* in this section.

Swats. In some places a newly brewed ale is called swats.

Sweet liquor. After the mashing in of the grain, the malt-sugar-laden water drawn from the tun goes by the name sweet liquor. After hops are added to the kettle, the name becomes wort.

Sweet stout. Another rendition of a full-bodied stout that evolved from Irish roots, sweet, or milk, stout was England's answer to Ireland's Irish or dry stout. Reducing the roasted barley, in its place English brewers substituted chocolate malt augmented with milk sugar (lactose). Yeast wouldn't ferment either of the new ingredients well, and thus sweet stout remained low in alcohol. In a way the modifications created dry stouts alter ego. Sweet stout lacks both the attractive luster of deep garnet clarity and the sharp flavors found in a dry stout. Instead, it steps forward with a sensuously dark concentration of full, thick-bodied malt. Brewers check its sweet intensity with a calculated balance of dark grains and hops that hold it comfortably short of cloying.

Swipes. A slang term for beer. At one time it also was applied to a thin or poor brew.

Takju. A Korean beer fermented from rice. Also spelled *yakju*.

Tannin. Also known as tannic acid it imparts a biting taste or sensation. The name brings to mind tannin's most profitable use—the tanning of animal hides. In wine, tannins assist in maturing the product. Less desirable in beer, tannins impart a sharp, astringent taste. If the brewer employs proper brewing techniques, tannins help clear the beer by combining with protein molecules and dropping out of the solution.

Tap-up Sunday. A regional celebration in England held on the Sunday before the second of October. During the 1600s and 1700s, tap-up Sunday was an occasion for anyone (regardless of license status) to tap and sell beer.

Teetotal. Along with teetotaler and teetotalism, all refer to the total abstinence from alcoholic beverages. Before it was corrupted, the root word T-totalism implied only the drinking of tea. Another explanation of the word comes from a temperance meeting in Hector, New York, in 1836, when members were identified by a badge that signified which pledge they took. Those observing an abstinence only from distilled spirits went by the original pledge, and they were marked with the letters O. P.: old pledge. Old pledgers didn't have it so bad—they could drink beer and keep their oath. Newer members pledged total abstinence and proudly wore the single letter T, which proclaimed them "total" abstainers. One source credits first use of the term to one Richard Turner of Preston, Lancashire, who gave in a speech before a temperance society in 1833 in which he used the term.

Temperance. Corrupted, twisted, and abused in modern meaning, temperance actually has a definition synonymous with moderation. Thus, when first applied to alcoholic beverages it was a way of talking about "good sense" drinking.

Temperance chart. Produced by Dr. Benjamin Rush, personal physician to George Washington, the chart recommended avoiding the debilitating effects of hard liquors and spirits but recommended the daily consumption of beer.

Thin. A beer with a lighter mouthfeel, typically a "smaller" beer.

T'ien tsiou. A name for the beerlike drinks made from millet throughout old China.

Tipple. "To drink slowly" was the original meaning, but later this word was used to identify any alcoholic beverage. Words closely associated with tipple include *tippler,* which describes a person engaged in slow but steady drinking, and *tippling,* the act of drinking slowly.

Tithe ales. In old England, a premium the church used as inducement for parishioners to pay their tithes. On the evening of Christmas Day the tithe-paying members of a church would gather for entertainment in the minister's chambers, with bread, cheese, and ale provided by the church.

Toeak. Described by some as a type of beer made in Bali, it is produced from the fermented sap of palm trees.

Toper. A person who habitually drinks to excess.

Toso. Japanese sake. The traditional version was infused with herbs. On the new year, toasts of *toso* ensure a long life free from evil.

Tosspot. In old England, a name for a drunkard.

Trappist. A beer brewed on the grounds of one of only six brewing abbeys in the world, five in Belgium and one in the Netherlands. The abbeys that may call their beers Trappist include Chimay, Rochefort, Orval, Westmalle, Westvletren, and Schapskoii. (These names refer to the name and location of the abbeys.) Other abbeys produce beers in this style under contract with commercial breweries, but these must be labeled either "abbey" or "Trappist style."

Monks in various European monasteries perfected brewing techniques and developed beer styles, among them the classic Trappist ales.

The beers of the Trappist or abbey style receive classifications similar to grades based upon the use they had in the monastery. Singles are beers that were traditionally served to common travelers and others visiting the monastery. Doubles are of a higher grade than the singles and were served to the brothers. Triples represents the highest quality beer and was reserved for the abbots, special guests, and special occasions.

Trinity audit. A college ale in old England, from Trinity College, Cambridge. College ales were provided to students on days of special note for the country and the college.

> *Oh in truth, it gladdens the heart to see*
> *What may spring from the Ale of Trinitie . . .*
> *Come back with the wisdom of mournful time,*
> *I'd labour—I'd toil—by night and day,*
> *(Mixing liquors and books away),*
> *Till I conquer'd that high and proud degree,*
> *M.A. (Master of Ale) of Trinitie.*

Colleges took equal pride in their ales and their academic achievements. See *college ales* in this section.

Tulipai. Another name for the beer of the Apache Indians. Also known as *oafka* and *tiswin*.

Two penny. English small beer of the seventeenth century. It cost two pennies per pint. It also represented one of the three beers used to make three threads, the forerunner of porter. See *porter* in this section.

Typyhle. The Old English word for ale.

Vatting. Though it's heard infrequently, vatting is another way to say blending.

Vertical tasting. A term applicable mostly to Belgian beers, old ales, and barley wines. To conduct a vertical tasting requires the gathering of a beer over the course of several different bottling years. Comparing the merits of each year proceeds vertically, through the bottles and time.

Vienna. Austria's greatest export, the style nearly vanished in the late 1800s but was saved by expatriate Austrians who continued to brew the style in their new home of Mexico. Vienna beers have an emphasis on malt, low hopping, medium body, a clean finish, toasty flavor, and attractive red hues. See *red beer* in this section.

Vienna beer as it was served in the 1800s.

Vinegar. A sour liquid resulting from acetic fermentation of any light alcohol. Producers of vinegar use wine, beer, or cider as a base. Each results in a distinctly different vinegar.

Waipiro. What New Zealanders called an attempt at a type of spruce beer made by Captain Cook while he was in New Zealand during 1773. He brewed the beer from molasses, which he added to the boiled branches of the manuka and rimu trees.

Wallup. English slang for a mild beer.

Warrington ale. An English regional beer that had loyal fans celebrating its character in song:

> *I've been crammed with good things like a wallet,*
> *And I've guzzled more drink than a whale;*
> *But the very best stuff to my palate*
> *Is a glass of your Warrington Ale.*

Weddyn ale. Brewed for the purpose of a wedding, weddÿn ale served a purpose identical to a bride ale. Newlywed brides at their receptions would exchange beer for a gift or cash contribution from the guests. The money raised assisted the new couple in beginning their life together.

Wheat beer. Imagine visiting Monticello as the guest of Thomas Jefferson. Mrs. Jefferson appears and asks if you'd like a beer. The one she hands you would be a wheat beer.

For centuries brewers have been making wheat beer. Brewers like Mrs. Jefferson made their beer with wheat for several reasons: It gave them more raw material for making beer, provided good "heading" properties, and made a very drinkable beer. These traits remain as important to brewers and beer drinkers today as they ever were.

Despite their resurgence in popularity, wheat beers remain a mystery to most Americans. Wheat beer is popular throughout Germany, and there are local differences in the style. Even the names vary: *weisse, weizen, hefeweizen.* Despite this, German wheat beers do share some common characteristics. Though German-style wheat beers come from the land of lagers, they fit securely in the ale category. Therefore, you'd expect to find fruity esters in the aroma, most commonly as the smell of banana. Adding to the aromatic complexity, a trace of clove supplies a spicy balance.

The heading comes from the high amount of protein in wheat, which breaks surface tension and produces a big, thick, creamy crown of foam. Of course, these protein molecules cause another easily observed trait—

haziness. Proteins are long molecules and have a length sufficient to refract light, thus wheat beers will appear quite hazy. However, some brewers use a filtering process that renders the beer bright and clear, especially in the American versions.

A layer of sediment in the bottom of the bottle also marks a wheat beer, most frequently in the hazy versions known as *hefeweizen.* When pouring a hefeweizen, Germans will leave a little beer in the bottle and swirl it to mix up the sediment, then pour it on top of the head. When consumed in this fashion the yeast provides an added side benefit, for it contains a significant amount of some B vitamins.

What about the taste? It too varies. The range of wheat beer runs from light to bubbly to tangy to malty and all combinations thereof. There are also dark (*dunkel weizen*) versions. The majority have considerable effervescence and a tangy palate. Because of the haze and layer of sediment, people sometimes mistakenly conclude that these beers have gone bad, but these are all desirable traits, derived from the protein and yeast. In fact, when you consider all the benefits of protein, brewers yeast, and vitamins in wheat beer, you could think of it as a health food.

For summer refreshment, the tangy character of wheat beer is a natural thirst quencher. Despite the variety, wheat beers do share one universal trait—they're a popular favorite of the summer months. A few of our favorites are Tabernash, Paulaner, and Schneider Weiss.

White ale. A beer made in England in the seventeenth and eighteenth centuries. Recipes included hops, flour, and spices. Eggs were added before fermenting (after the boil and cooling). A recipe of 1741 outlined the basic formulation: "The wort is brewed by the hostess, but the fermentation is brought on by the purchase of what they call 'ripening' or a composition, as some say, of flour of malt and whit of eggs . . ." The ale was described as milky-looking and there was speculation that it contained spice, milk, and gin. The recipe may remain a mystery, but all sources describe this as a beer with a short shelf life. It was made only in small batches for immediate consumption.

Whitsun ale. One of the many church and holiday ales, or celebrations, in old England. Whitsun ale commemorated the Whitsuntide holiday, a feast and celebration held in late spring as a special fund-raising event. It was described by one writer:

> Two young men of the parish are yerely chosen by their last Foregoers to be wardens, who, dividing the task, make collection among the parishoners. . . . This they employ in brewing . . . upon which holy days their neighbors meet at the Church-house, and there merrily . . . advance the churche's profit.

Wit. How do you become a brewing legend? The easiest way is to save a dying style, as Pierre Celis did with *wit* beer.

Originating in Belgium, wit evolved as a product of geography and world conquest. Belgium was part of the Netherlands in the early 1800s and was a wheat-growing region. The Dutch connection contributes the other major characteristic of wit. In that era the Dutch controlled the spice trade. Thus, coriander along with Curaçao orange peel from the Netherland Antilles and other spices found their way into the beer. The addition of spice wasn't by chance; rather, it derived from an older method of brewing practiced before the widespread use of hops.

In modern times wit beer fell from favor, and in 1954 the last of the wit breweries ceased operation. It was in 1966 that a Belgian, Pierre Celis, missing the old style, started producing his own version of wit called Hoegaarden, and eventually it regained favor.

Almost everything about wit beer is a bit different. It starts with a grain bill of 45–50 percent unmalted wheat. This does two things: It provides a very white, dense, rocky head, and a cloudy, hazy beer. The haze is a direct result of the high protein content in wheat. Belgians proudly flaunt this cloudiness and leave the finished beer unfiltered. Some versions also use a small amount of oats, amounting to about 5 percent, to add a touch of silky mouthfeel. Like other beers of Belgium, wit uses aged hops, so there are very low levels of hops in both taste and aroma. What is noticeable are the spices, a harmony of sophisticated sublimity. You should be able to identify clearly the orange and coriander, along with other spices favored by individual brewers. Wit should be, in the finer versions, well balanced. You may also detect notes of honey and apple as by-products of the wheat, and perhaps a trace of the horse-blanket quality described as "house character" in many Belgian beers. They do not exhibit any of the banana or clove notes of their German cousins. Bottled within four to five days of primary fermentation, wits have a lactic character that diminishes as the beer ages into a soft, slightly sweet profile.

Pierre relocated to Austin, Texas, and grateful fans have embraced the American version as much as the people of Belgium popularized the original. In fact, the beer-loving citizens of his native country have bestowed on Pierre a bit of an honor. You can find Celis wit in bars all over Belgium.

Withdrawals. Trade word of the seventeenth and eighteenth centuries that was used in England and identified the amount of beer upon which excise taxes were calculated, as such it was an equivalent measure of sales.

Wood. Mostly a British term, it originated when most beer came from casks and refers to any unbottled beer. Phrases such as *beer from the wood* and *beer in the wood* refer to drinking "real beer" served directly from a cask. Some beer drinkers insist that the only beer worth drinking comes from wooden casks. Others point out that beer served in that manner quickly turns sour and undrink-

Old revelers enjoying a beer from the wood.

able. What's the best advice? If offered a freshly tapped cask beer cared for by a knowledgeable and attentive cellar, give it a try.

X. A designation applied to beer and ale, it was thought to have started in one of two ways. One theory advocates this was a designation of quality. Xs were placed on casks by a monastery in the days when most people were illiterate, and the higher the number of Xs, the greater the quality of the brew. Another theory supports the idea that the practice was introduced later, when excise officers marked casks as an indication of the duty imposed, the higher the number, the stronger the beer, and the higher the tax.

Yakju. A rice-based beerlike drink of Korea. Also spelled *takju*.

Yeast bite. The yeasty taste in a beer from poor decanting or from a hastily racked beer that carried too much yeast. The flavor closely parallels the smell of brewers yeast.

Zichus. Latin word for a beverage fermented after performing a decoction of barley and water. In other words—beer.

Zitos. The Greek word for beer.

Zumzammin. Of biblical origin, this was a large goatskin pouch used for holding beer and other liquids.

Zur. An old rye- and oat-based beer of eastern Europe and Russia.

Zuur. The class of somewhat sour brown and red beers of Belgium.

Zymurgy. The study of fermentation, also known as zymology.

Zythos. Ancient Greek name for barley wine that came from the older Egyptian word *zythum*.

Zythum. Egyptian barley wine dating to the time of the pharaohs. An old recipe started with soaking in water a loaf of crude grain bread with dates and flavored with juniper, ginger, cumin, and assorted berries.

Beer-Based Mixed Drinks

omehow the delegates of the Constitutional Convention managed to put regional interests aside during that sweltering summer of 1787 and forge a new government. As the president of the convention swung his gavel to close the proceedings he already knew where they were headed. The representatives were beer drinkers and with the business at hand finished, George Washington and the Constitutional Convention adjourned to Philadelphia's City Tavern for a drink, and to many it was for a mixed drink.

Ale provided the base for most of the cocktails enjoyed by beer drinker's during the colonial period. Added to beer's regular consumption, its use in mixed drinks was a factor in the growth of brewing.

One of the most popular beer-based mixed drinks was the "flip." John Adams, the delegate of Massachusetts and second president of the United States, reported that a person spending a day in a tavern would find it full of people drinking drams of flip, carousing, and swearing. Flip was primarily an American drink, although the English drank it as well. The earliest mention of flip is thought to be in 1690, but the first reference in print was the December 1704 edition of the *New England Almanac*:

> *The days are short, the weather's cold,*
> *By tavern fires tales are told.*
> *Some ask for dram when first come in,*
> *Others with flip and bounce begin.*

Orders of flip often punctuated the entries in General George Washington's expense account, and General Israel Putnam had his own well-regarded recipe. Almost anywhere a revolutionary fire was burning a loggerhead (an instrument used to stir the fire) stood by the ready.

Sometimes loggerheads were referred to as hottle or flip-dog. It was such a common and well-loved fireplace instrument it inspired James Lowell to pen the following lines of praise:

> *Where dozed a fire of beechen logs that bred*
> *Strange fancies in its embers golden—red,*
> *And nursed the loggerhead, whose hissing dip,*
> *timed by wise instinct, creamed the bowl of flip*

A variation on the flip theme was when a fresh egg was beaten into the mixture. In this case it was considered different enough to earn the separate name of *bellowstop*. As the loggerhead hit this mixture it foamed over the mug and most likely the rest of the table. Flip was so widely ordered and such a fashionable drink that it was in demand well into the mid-1800s.

Although flip was certainly one of the most common beer mixtures, it was by no means the only drink ordered by thirsty firebrands (colonists). One curious mixed drink was the "whistle-belly-vengeance." It was the absolute rage in Salem, Massachusetts. To make the whistle-belly-vengeance required that the tavern keeper have a batch of sour household beer, simmered in a kettle and sweetened with molasses. Crumbs of "ryneinjun" bread were added to thicken the brew, which was served piping hot. The recipe was common enough for Dean Swift to mention it in his "Polite Conversations":

> *Hostess (offering ale to Sir John Linger):*
> I never taste malt liquor, but they say ours is well hopp'd.
> *Sir John:* Hopp'd why if it had hopp'd a little further,
> it would have hopp'd into the river.
> *Hostess:* I was told ours was very strong.
> *Sir John:* Yes! Strong of water. I believe the brewer forgot the malt,
> or the river was too near him. Faith! it is more whip-belly-vengeance;
> he that drinks most has the worst share.

With an endorsement such as this is it any wonder whistle-belly-vengeance was also known by the name whip-belly-vengeance. Thankfully this drink was a fad that faded away.

Another favored mixed drink was "calibogus" or "bogus." Consisting of rum and unsweetened beer, this drink was the colonial version of today's boilermaker, which consists of whiskey and beer. Yet another drink was "mumm"—a flat ale made of oat and wheat malt.

If all this didn't tickle a colonist's fancy, or if it was just a case of boredom with the usual beer-based drinks, you could try a flip that used cider instead of beer. The other possibility was a mixture called "ebulum"—a cider-based punch in which the cider was mixed with the juices of elder and juniper berries. One New England favorite, "black strap," didn't use beer at all; it mixed cold rum and molasses. Casks of this were found in most every general store. Next to the store's barrels of black strap were hung dried, salted cod fish, which the customers could munch for free. Of course there was a charge for a drink when all that salt made the customers thirsty!

Though we often long for the simplicity of the early days, it would seem songwriter Billy Joel may have hit the nail on the head when he wrote "the good old days weren't always good." Even today's worst beer seems pretty tame in comparison to these.

Ale-brue. In old England, spiced ale, later called aleberry.

Aleberry. Also spelled aleberries, aylesbury, ale-brue, and alesbury. No berries were used in making this beer. It was an old term (1600s) derived from a combination of the words for "ale" and "bre" (broth). It was made of ale that was hopped, as opposed to the earlier form of beer, which was not.

Their ale-berries, cawdles and possets each one,
And sullabubs made at the milking pail,
Although they be many, Beer comes not in any
But all are composed with a Pot of Good Ale.

Aleberry was actually a type of drink, gruel, or soup made with warm ale, oatmeal, sugar, bread, and various spices that commonly included lemon juice and nutmeg.

Ale flip. A favored English and American mixed beer drink of the 1700s. See *flip* in this section. When first in use, the word described all hot beer–based drinks; later, it described any drink made with ale, crushed ice, and an egg.

Ale-gill. An old English mixed drink in which ale was flavored with ground ivy. (Please do not try this at home!) The type of ivy used was ale-hoof. See *alehoof* in the Beer and Beer Drinking section.

Ale nog. As the name implies, this is an ale-based egg nog. The original recipe calls for four coffeespoons of milk, sugar, eight egg yolks, and nutmeg—all well mixed and beaten to a froth. Then, slowly fold in a quart of beer or ale.

Ale posset. Through the early 1700s English drinkers could often be heard ordering posset. To us this would be unimaginable, because this drink was made from a foul-sounding combination of warm curdled milk added to ale and flavored with nutmeg. See *posset* and *egg posset* in this section.

Ale punch. See *punch* in this section.

Apperley's mixture. Popular in Australia in the 1850s, this was a cocktail made of ale, ginger beer, mint, and sugar. It is to be hoped the effect of the whole was greater than the sum of the parts.

Apple Florentine. Does any beer-based drink sound more elegant? This was a dessert.

> According to parental tradition, this "Florentine" consisted of an immensely large dish of pewter, or such like metal, filled with "good baking apples," sugar, and lemon, to the very brim, with a roll of rich paste as a covering—pie fashion. When baked, and before serving up, the "upper crust" or "lid," was taken off by a "skilful" hand and divided into sizeable triangular portions or shares, to be again returned into the dish, ranged in formal "order round" by way of a garnish; when to complete the mess, a full quart of well-spiced ale was poured in, quite hot, hissing hot. . . .
>
> *(W. T. Marchant, "In Praise of Ale")*

It was quite fashionable to serve the apple Florentine in the winter months.

B & B. In England this was one of many mixtures of different beers. It was reported to have been made by mixing a tankard with one part Burton ale and one part bitter.

Balderdash. Understood by most to signify nonsense, the word originated as a term that indicated a worthless mixture of drinks, such as a combination of beer and wine.

Bang. Composed of spiced warm ale, cider, and whiskey, bang was one of scores of beer drinks laced with alcohol. Undoubtedly the name comes either from the manner in which it hit the drinker or the first thing the drinker heard upon awakening.

Beer buster. This beer-based mixed drink was made with a jigger of vodka and a dash of Tabasco® sauce in a highball glass. Beer filled the remaining space in the glass.

The hazards of drinking beer cups *as portrayed in "Modern Midnight Converstaion" by Hogarth.*

Beer cup. Beer lovers of old England made this refreshing drink as follows: Take a quart of mild ale, add a glass of white wine, a glass of brandy, one glass of capillaire (a sweetened syrup), the juice of a lemon and a thin slice of its peel, grated nutmeg, and a piece of bread. Also known as cool tankard.

Beer saints. Strongly linked with beer and brewing in the Middle Ages, the Catholic Church has many beer saints. See *saints* in the Beer and Beer Drinking section.

Bellowstop. A warm colonial beer-based drink with an egg mixed in. See *flip* in this section.

Berliner Weisse mit Strippe. A glass of Berliner *weisse* (the classic Berlin version of German wheat beer—tart and effervescent) served with a tall slender glass of Kummel spirits.

Bismarck. Said to be of German origin, this beer-based drink contains equal parts Champagne and stout. Why waste good stout? See *black velvet* in this section.

Black and Tan. Originally reputed to be a mixture either of stout with mild ale or porter with beer, Black and Tan now implies a stout and ale mixture. During the 1920s the name was a reference to the uniforms worn by the occupying English troops in Ireland.

Black velvet. The English version of what Germans call a Bismarck, this is a beer-based cocktail made of equal portions of stout and Champagne. Customarily the stout would be floated on top of the Champagne.

Blow my skull off. A most appropriate name for the effect created by this stout-based mixed drink. Other ingredients include rum, cayenne pepper, lime juice, assorted herbs, and opium. For obvious reasons, government authorities may demonstrate concern if you try to faithfully duplicate this drink. It originated in Australia.

Boilermaker. When first used, the term described a beer with salt added that was served to boilermakers and others in occupations involving high heat. The drink was a way to replace the salt lost during heavy work. Later, "boilermaker" referred to whiskey followed by a beer chaser.

Borage. An herb with blue-starred shaped flowers. Leaves are sometimes used in salads. In beer it is applied in the same manner as are other herbs and spices.

Bragget. Also spelled as bracket and braggon. Dating back to the 1600s in England, this was a spiced ale sweetened with honey. When used to describe a modern version, the word describes a beer to which cinnamon, cloves, and honey are added.

Bragot. A drink of the Welsh, similar to bragget. It was made from beer sweetened with honey and spiced with cinnamon and galingale (a type of reed).

Brasenose ale. Reported by different sources as a mixed beer drink, with additions of sugar and roasted apples.

Brewage. An archaic term for "mixed drink." The vast majority of the earliest mixed drinks were beer-based; thus, the origin of this word presents no mystery.

Broadway. A Japanese beer cocktail mixed with equal amounts of beer and cola.

Brown Betty. A mixed beer drink that is served hot, this one is made from hot ale to which are added brandy, spices, and a piece of toast.

Brown velvet. A derivation of the black velvet or Bismarck, but still more unlikely. In this version stout serves as a base to which port wine is added. It might go down easy, but it sure sounds like a guaranteed hangover.

Brutole. A general term for a medicinal beer. Any number of spices and herbs have been added to beer in producing concoctions intended as cures. Practice of such beer mixing was common from the days of the ancient Egyptians to recent times. In fact, the Egyptian Book of the Dead listed at least one hundred beer-based remedies. For example: To guard against death, mix the foam of a beer with half an onion. It makes you wonder whether it worked because no one ever got close enough to pass along an infection.

Burton soda. A mixed drink of English origins made from equal parts ale and ginger beer.

Buttered ale. Also known as buttered beer, this English drink reached the height of its popularity in the 1500s. It was originally made in the days before hops were added to beer; thus, a buttered ale was a strong, unhopped beer to which were added sugar, spices, butter, and an egg yolk. No doubt this was a forerunner of the colonial beer drink called flip.

Calibogus. Also called bogus, this was a drink consisting of equal parts rum and unsweetened beer. It was popular in colonial New England, where rum was a plentiful product.

Caudle. A gruel-based beverage, served hot, to which beer, wine, or spirits were added.

Cool tankard. Synonymous with beer cup, this was one of the many "cups" (drinks) popular in the 1600s in England. To make a cool tankard, take the juice of the peel of one lemon, extracted by rubbing the peel on a loaf of sugar, thinly slice two additional lemons, add one-fourth pound of sugar, a half pint of brandy, and a quart of cold water. After mixing the ingredients in a large jug, pour in one pint of white wine and a quart of strong beer, ale, perry, or cider. Sweeten to taste with capillaire or sugar, add a handful of balm and another of borage, ice the jug down, and let it sit for one hour.

Cooper. An old English beer drink made from equal portions of porter and stout. See *cooper* in the Beer Bottles, Barrels, Glasses, Vessels, and Measures section.

Copus. A drink prepared from beer, wine, and spices that is served hot. To prepare copus, heat two cups of ale, add four wineglasses of brandy, three wineglasses of noyau (a liquor with fruit kernels added), a pound of lump sugar, the juice of one lemon, a piece of toast, a dozen cloves, and a little nutmeg.

Cramabull. An old beverage from the seventeenth and eighteenth centuries made by warming beer, sweetening it, fortifying it with rum, and adding beaten raw eggs. It was served warm.

Cups. Dating back centuries, the expression *cups* has been eliminated from the American vernacular, but in other countries it remains in use as a word for a mixed drink. Cups contained watered-down beer, wine, or spirits. Routinely a summer drink, cups was often spiced with mint, citrus, or other fruit. No set recipe existed—people concocted their own favorite blends. The Duchess of Saint Albans was reported to have a recipe she called The Ale of Health and Strength, which allegedly was small beer into which she boiled a majority of the herbs from her garden. Verse written about cups in general provides advice as to its consumption:

> *Three cups of this a prudent man may take;*
> *The first of these for constitutions sake,*
> *The second to the girl he loves the best,*
> *The third and last to lull him to rest.*

Other popular cups had names such as Humpty Dumpty, clamberclown, hugmatee, stickback, cock ale, stiffe, blind pinneaux, stephony, northdown, and knock-me-down.

Curatives. Beer has supplied the base for curative tonics throughout history. Translations of the remedies listed in the ancient Egyptian Book of the Dead identify over one hundred recipes based on beer. Ben Jonson in *The Alchemist*, written in the 1500s, noted the effect of ale in medicine of the period: "Yes, faith, she dwells in Sea-coal lane, did cure me With sodden ale." Other sources listed countless remedies, some of the more curious "medications" relieved suffering from:

Black jaundice. To prepare a cure required a base made from a pint of honey and a gallon of ale. To that was added about a half cup of red nettles and some saffron and then the mixture was boiled. It was skimmed as it boiled, strained, and cooled. Over a period of two weeks it was administered to the patient every morning.

Consumption. Recommended in *The London County Brewer* of 1744, a brown ale called "stich" was administered to unfortunates suffering from consumption. It was brewed from the first running off the malt and thereby was of considerable strength.

Coughs. Add a handful of red sage to a quart of ale and boil it, strain, and then add a quarter pound of treacle. Consume warm immediately before bed.

Coughs and shortness of wind. A popular cure for coughs was buttered beer. To prepare a batch, take a quart of strong beer and add a good piece of fresh butter, sugar candy, licorice, and grated ginger. See buttered beer in this section.

For good against the devil. Mix a handful of sedge and gladden in a pan, pour in a bowlful of ale, boil the mixture and "rub" in twenty-five libcorns.

Hiccups. Pound the root of jarrow, work it into a good beer, and serve it to the patient lukewarm. This was also alleged to be effective against all manner of other internal disturbances.

Lunacy. Work herbs into clear ale, say seven masses over the worts, add garlic and holy water, then have the patient suffering from lunacy drink it out of a church bell.

Lung disease. Patients were to avoid drinking sweet ale; however, they were prescribed a clear ale in which young oak rind was boiled.

Pains in the knees. Muddled (pounded and mixed) woodwax and hedge-rife, which were then added to ale. A remedy devised by the Saxons, this was applied both internally and externally.

Restorative for those low with sickness. The following remedy was suggested:

Take two pounds of dates and wash them clean in ale, then cut them and take out the stones and white skins, then cut them small, and beat them in a mortar, till they begin to work like wax, and then take a quart of clarified Honey or sugar, and a half an ounce of the Podder of Long Pepper, as much of Mace of Cloves, Nutmegs, and Cinnamon, of each one Drachm, as much of the Powder of Lignum Aloes; beat all the Spies together and Seeth the Dates with the sugar or Honey with an easie fire, and let it seeth . . . then eat little every morning and evening . . . and it will renew and restore.

(Book of Notable Things *[late 1500s])*

Dark and stormy. From Bermuda comes this mind-numbing mixture of ginger beer and rum. Give some to a group of tourists on the beach, then sit back to enjoy the show.

Depth bomb. When referring to beer, it has a meaning nearly identical to the depth charge: a shot or jigger of whiskey dropped into a large glass of beer. However, in some areas a cocktail of applejack, brandy, grenadine, and lemon juice is called a depth bomb.

Depth charge. A variation of the boilermaker, this is a shot of schnapps added to a glass of beer. The method of adding the schnapps gives the drink its name, for the drinker drops the shot glass of schnapps into the beer glass.

Dog's nose. Once a fashionable beer cocktail, this was a variation of the warm beer drink theme. At first glance it may seem curious that it called for an addition of gin, but this was the period of gin's rising popularity in England. To make dog's nose, ale was heated and fortified with gin and sugared to taste. Later versions substituted porter for ale.

Donaldson's beer cup. One of the lighter interpretations of a beer cup, this was made of one pint of ale to which the peel of one-half lemon was added, then a half liquor glass of noyau (a liquor with fruit kernels added), a bottle of seltzer water, a little nutmeg and sugar, and some ice.

Dr. Brown's ale. A popular beer composition intended as a cure, it was made by infusing ale with various spices and medicines. It was invented by Dr. Brown, the court physician to King James I of England. His recipe specified everything he thought necessary to rid a patient of coughs and other aliments:

> Take Senna and Polypedium, each four ounces, Sarseperilla two ounces, Agrimony and Maidenhair of each a small handful, scurvy grass a quarter of a peck, bruise them grossly in a stone mortar, put them into a thin canvass bag, and hang the bag in nine or ten gallons of ale; when it is well worked and when it is three or four days old, it is ripe enough to be drawn off and bottled, or as you see fit.

The illiterate general public knew they could purchase this cure wherever a tavern sign displayed an image of "The Butlers Head."

Ebulum. An ale-based drink prepared with a mixture of juniper, ginger, elderberries, and spices. Also known as ebulam. To make a batch at home, try the old recipe:

> *In a hogshead of the first and strongest wort was boiled one bushel*
> *of ripe elderberries. The wort was then strained and, when cold,*
> *worked in a hogshead. Having lain in cask for about a year it was bottled.*
> *Some persons added an infusion of hops by way of preservative*
> *and some likewise hung a small bag of bruised spices in the vessel.*
>
> *(Bickerdyke [1889])*

Another version, white ebulum, was made from pale malt and white elderberries.

Egg hot. Spiced beer mixed with eggs was very popular from the mid-seventeenth to late eighteenth centuries. An egg hot was made from one pint of "good ale," to which three eggs, two ounces of sugar, nutmeg, and ginger were added. Typically, egg recipes called for using half the beer as a base, to which the other ingredients were added while heating. When the first mixture was blended, the remaining beer was added and the drink was served immediately.

Egg posset. A variation of the familiar "egg and beer" theme. An old recipe for egg posset outlines a procedure to

> Beat up well the yolks of eight eggs with refined sugar pulverized and a nutmeg grated; then extract the juice from the rind of a lemon by rubbing loaf sugar upon it, and put the sugar with a piece of cinnamon and a quart of strong home-brewed beer into a saucepan, place it on the fire, and when it boils take it off, then add a single glass of gin, or this may be left out, put the liquor into a spouted jug, and pour it gradually among the yolks of eggs, &c. All must be kept well stirred with a spoon while the liquor is being poured in. If it be not sweet enough add loaf sugar. In the university this beverage is frequently given to servants at Christmas and other high festivals.

Eggy-hot. A Cornish rendition of the egg hot and egg posset, it was a mixture made from a base of heated beer with eggs, rum, and spices. Immediately after all the ingredients were combined it was poured from jug to jug until it foamed and was served warm.

Entire. See *porter* in the Beer and Beer Drinking section.

Flap-dragon. A beer drink popular in England and colonial America from the 1600s to mid-1700s made with any number of flammable liquids floating on top of the beer. Immediately before consumption the spirits were set afire and the mixture was consumed in one draft, thus extinguishing the flame as it went down. In some regions raisins and other edibles were included and were also consumed while ablaze.

Flip. Served hot, this was a fortified beer-based drink, which required eggs in the preparation. The most common recipe from the 1600s to mid-1700s called for:

> A great mug or pitcher filled two-thirds full of strong ale; sweeten with sugar or molasses and flavor with a gill—of rum. Into this mixture thrust a hot loggerhead.

Another recipe:

> Place in a pan one quart strong ale together with sugar rubbed over the rind of a lemon, and cinnamon. Remove from heat when boiling, add one pint cold ale. Beat the yolks of six eggs with powdered sugar and grated nutmeg. Pour the hot ale mixture from the pan into the eggs, stirring them while so doing. Pour the mixture as swiftly as possible from one vessel to the other until a white froth appears. Then add one or two wine glasses of gin or rum.

Some modified the basic recipe by beating a fresh egg into the mixture. That change was considered different enough to earn the separate name of bellowstop. As the loggerhead hit the mixture it foamed over the mug and most likely the rest of the table. What could be more fun than sitting around a fire in the taproom and ordering drinks you knew would cause a big mess? Flip was so widely ordered and such a fashion that it was a hit well into the mid-1800s.

Foggerty. Anchor Brewing Company provides everything needed to mix a foggerty. Simply add equal parts of Liberty Ale and Old Foghorn to a glass. Does it result in a fortified Liberty or an extra hoppy Foghorn? Who cares? (In some parts of the San Francisco Bay Area foggerty goes by the name *Paul Revere's last ride,* in reference to the date Anchor first released Liberty Ale—1976.)

Foggy night in the Sierra. A variation of the foggerty, this drink uses Anchor Brewing's Old Foghorn mixed with Sierra Nevada pale ale.

Freemason's cup. Potent and dangerous, freemason's cup sounds more like a liquid paint remover than beer. Take one pint of Scotch ale, another of mild, add one-half pint of brandy, a pint of sherry, half a pound of loaf sugar, and a generous amount of ground nutmeg. Drink at night close to the bed. Guaranteed to produce a headache the following morning.

Ginger beer. A beer-based mixed drink, it may take the form of any item in a nearly endless list of variations. One recipe calls for a beer base (three parts beer) to which is added one part Champagne, one part ginger ale, one part *framboise,* and a dash of powdered ginger. See *ginger beer* in the Beers and Beer Drinking section.

Grace cup. When used to describe a mixed beer drink in the 1600s and 1700s, (see *cups* in this section), grace cup was commonly featured as a beverage at corporation dinners in England. One recipe listed ingredients and a procedure that read:

> Extract the juice from the peeling of a lemon and cut the remainder into thin slices; put it into a jug or bowl, and pour on it three half pints of strong home-brewed beer and a [cup] of mountain wine: grate a nutmeg into it; sweeten it to your taste; stir it till the sugar is dissolved, and then add three or four slices of bread toasted brown. Let it stand two hours, and then strain off into the Grace Cup.

Granny. A beer drink of the United Kingdom, that is now somewhat out of favor. It's made by mixing old and mild ale, an idea similar in nature to a foggerty. Indeed, granny would like that!

Half and half. Debate surrounds the true makeup of a half and half. The truth—it's only beer. You'd be correct in calling any mixture of beers from within the same general family (poured in equal parts) by the name. For example: a mix of mild and bitter, or a mix of pale ale and stout, or pale ale and porter would be a half and half. Some insist only specific beer styles should be used, most frequently lager and stout are mentioned. It would seem such rigidity borders on fascism, then again, maybe they bought shorts a little too tight.

Het beer. A Scottish beer drink bringing together whiskey, ale, and raw eggs. Could it have started as Scottish humor?

Holiday beers. Holiday ales and beers have become a popular rage over the last few years as micros bring forth their interpretation of a holiday gift to beer enthusiasts. There's even a way to make your own. But first, where did all this business of putting herbs, fruits, and spices in beer start? Back in the days before hops made their debut as a beer preservative, that is, earlier than A.D. 800 or so, brewers often resorted to mixes of herbs, spices, and even tree bark and peppers to help stabilize their brews. How this came to represent the taste of the winter solstice is a different story.

Way back in our collective past the seeds of winter celebrations were planted by the ancient Romans. As days became short, the Romans honored and toasted the god Saturn with feasts, parties, and celebrations known as Saturnalia (there's even ale in the name). Although the ancient Romans are most associated with wine, their records are filled with references to beer. Other early cultures also celebrated the coming of winter. The Norse reveled each year as they approached the longest night. In their folklore, diminutive mythical spirits called *yule* dominated this season. In the tenth century the Norwegian king Hakon the Good wrestled with being a good Christian while longing for the simpler days of the pagan festivals. What better compromise than to simply proclaim that both should be celebrated simultaneously as a single feast? As for the length of these combined holidays, he thought it only fitting that they should last as long as the beer flowed.

During the fifth century in Britain a local overlord by the name of Vortigern played, by some accounts, a part in the Wassail tradition. According to the legend, his Saxon subjects presented him a bowl of ale during a feast in his honor, with the proclamation "Louerd king woes hoeil." Of course, Vortigern didn't know the meaning of the phrase, which translates to "Lord king your health." But when he inquired, the Saxons explained, "It is the custom of the Saxons that friend says to friend, 'Wassail' and the other says 'Drinc Hail.'" Eventually the term was related to the merry-making around the holidays.

King Arthur had his own toast for this time of year. His Waes-Hael got right to the point:

> *Waes-Hael! for Lord and Dame*
> *O! merry be their Dole;*
> *Drink-hael! in Jesus name,*
> *And fill the tawny bowl.*

It seemed only natural to warm a cold winter night with a strong ale. As time passed, the holiday ale met the offspring of yule, a spiced loaf called yule cake. A slice of this was placed in a bottom of a bowl, and warm ale floated it up toward the brim. The cup would be passed around with much merriment until both the ale and yule cake were gone. Then it was a simple matter of mixing another, and another until all were gloriously incapacitated.

To help you join in on this old custom, here's one of the original recipes. Get a large bowl, dump a half pound of sugar in the bottom, pour in a pint of warm beer, add a sprinkling of nutmeg and ginger (grated), and mix in four glasses of sherry. Top it off by adding five pints of beer. Allow this to sit for a few hours, and just before serving float a few thin slices of toast on top along with a few slices of lemon.

All that sounds good enough, but it might be simpler just to buy a modern equivalent already brewed and bottled. Some beer experts will cite porters or Belgian beers as the toughest style to nail down, but in reality it's the winter warmer, also known as holiday ale, that challenges description. Normally a brewer strives for consistency in styles; deviations are usually subtle. Winter warmers are different—they seem to embrace diversity. In a brewery's standard beer this irregularity would be unacceptable, but it's almost expected in holiday beers. Nearly every brewery's version varies from year to year, but despite this variance the profiles of a particular rendition generally remain constant. Winter beers tend to be stronger than their year-round counterparts. They are usually of dark amber color and may include spices of nutmeg, cinnamon, clove, ginger, licorice, molasses, and others. Higher alcohol levels and spices result in good storage properties, and holiday versions placed in cool, dark storage will remain drinkable at the next year's holiday.

When serving a winter warmer, cellaring temperatures of about 50–55 °F are best for releasing the bouquet. Use a snifter or bowl-shaped glass to capture and savor the aromatics. Then it's a simple matter of placing another log on the fire and settling back to enjoy both the season and the beer. But don't wait too long. As the ad for Geary's winter beer says, "Only available while the weather sucks!"

Hot pot. Heated spirits and warmed ale, once popular in England and rather like a hot boilermaker. Heated, it would get into your system even faster—what a great idea. Also called hum and ruddle.

Huckle-my-buff. English mixologists seem to have a curious fascination with eggs, which appears to know no boundaries. Huckle-my-buff combines eggs with hot beer and brandy.

Hum. This was once a widespread generic name for a heated ale-and-beer mixture. It was sold in small measures and served in a "hum glass." Mentioned in the Elizabethan playwrights' Beaumont and Fletcher's *The Wild Goose Chase*, it appeared there as a quote in the passage: "What a cold I have over my stomach; would I'd some hum."

Considered to wield an above-average impact, hum was always mentioned as containing a potency worthy of respect. Supposedly, consuming enough would make your brain hum. Also called hot pot and ruddle.

Hungerford Park. Recommended as an excellent hot-weather drink, this was a type of beer cup the inventor recommended for "shooting parties"! Blend one by cutting apples into slices and dropping them into a jug. Add the peel and juice of one lemon and grate in a dash of fresh nutmeg. Next, pour in three bottles of ginger beer, a half pint of sherry, two and a quarter pints of draft ale, sweeten to taste with sifted loaf sugar dissolved by stirring, and let the jug stand in ice. One drinker, identified only as Colonel B., advised adding a half bottle of Champagne, which makes it "awful good." See *cups* in this section.

Irish Picon. A blend of stout, amer picon (a fortified French wine), and lemon zest added to a large tumbler of ice.

Island grog. Heat Pilsener beer to slightly below its boiling point. Add one large spoonful of white rum and four large spoonfuls of powdered sugar to the heated beer, stir to dissolve, and serve piping hot.

Jingle. Holidays bring out a large number of traditional beer mixed drinks. Jingle's recipe calls for ale sweetened with sugar and flavored with nutmeg and apples. Jingle was reported to have a taste that closely resembled lamb's wool. It sounds innocuous, but drinking enough of it will ring your bell.

Julep. Well known as a bourbon-based drink of the United States. Historically, the name originated well before its use in America. Samuel Pepys wrote of it in 1660, describing it as "a sweet drought" designed to disguise an unpleasant medicine. Although he did not provide the recipe, it was most likely one of the health cups made from beer and intended as a remedy.

Lager and lime. A drink of England similar in nature to the shandy, it employs lager flavored with lime juice. An English version of the Corona-with-lime craze of the 1980s.

Lamb's wool. Also spelled lambswool. Wintertime in England had the greatest number of mixed beer drinks. Among them was lamb's wool. Dating to the 1700s it was part of the festivities held on the first of November to celebrate the harvest of fruits and seeds. It was traditionally served from that point through the winter season as a form of strong drink.

> *Doubt not, then said the King, my promist secresye:*
> *The King shall never know more on't for mee.*
> *A cupp of lambswool they dranke unto him then,*
> *And to their bedds they past presentlie.*

Tavern owners and others prepared Lambswool by warming a strong (old) ale while mixing in nutmeg (grated), ginger, and sugar. Apples were roasted separately until their skins burst and were added to the warm beer mixture immediately before serving.

Light-and-mild. Equal amounts of pale ale and mild mixed through the process of pouring and served chilled.

Lüttje lage. German beer drink in which a shot of schnapps and a beer combine in a cocktail traditionally downed in one long draft. Think of it as a German version of the boilermaker.

Madureria. Why anyone would want to mix beer and wine remains a complete mystery. Of all the many combinations, the hardest to comprehend might be the madureria, a mixture of chilled Pilsener and Madeira wine served in a tall glass.

Midnight fog. Reportedly invented on Lake Powell, Utah, this drink's ingredients must have been imported. It consists of a blend of Anchor Brewing's Old Foghorn and porter. Think of it as porter with a punch.

Mild and bitter. A blend of ales or beers, in its original form it was made half of beer (beer as it was known in the old definition, as an unhopped and mild ale) and half of ale (hopped and bitter).

Milk ale. Not a beer made from milk, this was another of the drinks with beer as a base. To make one, heat one quart of ale with a pinch each of grated dried ginger and nutmeg. While heating slowly, stir in one large spoonful of sugar. In a separate pan heat a quart of milk to just below boiling, then add it to the ale mixture and serve warm. See *syllabub* in this section.

Moscow mule. Reportedly a mixed drink made by combining vodka, ginger beer, and lime. Some vodkas possess a strong taste and aroma, and mixing makes them more palatable.

Mother-in-law. An English name used to describe the popular barroom practice of mixing equal parts of bitter and stout. Some writers reported this drink as equal portions of stout and beer. In all examples stout was common, and regardless of the other ale or beer used, this drink sounds like another name for a half and half.

Mould ale. Served hot, this is a spiced ale that was customarily prepared for funeral services in England during the 1600s. A close relative of mulled ale.

Muddle. Old mixed beer recipes called for blends of herbs, leaves, and spices added as flavoring to beer. In order to mix them thoroughly they were often crushed, or muddled.

Mugwort. Once popular in England, this was a beer flavored with artemisia (a variety of herbal shrub with strong-smelling foliage). See *wormwood* in this section.

Mull. Dating from the time when warm drinks were popular in England and its colonies, mulled (heated) drinks were thought more easily absorbed by, and healthier for, the human body.

> *But all with sweeter mulled ale,*
> *Pass gaily life's sweet stream along,*
> *With interlude of ancient song—*
> *And as each rosy cup they drain,*
> *Bounty replenishes again.*

A common characteristic was the warm preparation and consumption. Variety came from the addition of other ingredients to the base of beer. Spices and sugar were the most frequently used flavorings, and eggs and fruit were also used.

Multum. A flavoring for old beer-based mixed drinks, multum was a combination of quassia (a bitter substance from the tree of the same name) and licorice. Some renditions contained cochineal (a red organic dye), which was called "hard multum."

Mumm. Don't be deceived by the name, this had nothing to do with Champagne. In fact, it's hard to imagine a drink further removed. Mumm was a charming flat ale made of oat and wheat malt. Thought by many to be a mixed beer drink, it is actually brewed with a great number of ingredients to create that effect. Originally made in Brunswick (Braunschweig), Germany, in 1489, its creation has been credited to Christian Mumme, thus the name. See *mumm* in the Beer and Beer Drinking section.

Nuts and bolts. One of the interesting names substituted for the more dry, and general, term of half and half. Nuts and bolts specifically refers to the mixing of equal parts of mild and bitter. Each taste complements the other, rather as if fitting a nut to a bolt.

Old and mild. English mixed drink that contained portions of both old (strong) ale and mild. Another report insisted old and mild was a mix of mild ale and Burton ale with the "old" reflecting Burton-on-Trent's status as an old brewing center.

Old trousers. Inexpensive usually does mean cheap, and none could have been cheaper than old trousers. Now outlawed, the drink was once served in London taverns. As customers left partially consumed beers during the day, at closing the barkeep would collect the dregs and mix them together for resale. On the next day the bar would have a new stock of "old trousers for sale." See *heel taps* and *hamsters* in the Beer Bottles, Barrels, Glasses, Vessels, and Measures section.

Panache. Few beer mixed drinks survived into the modern era, but *panache* is one that has. Made of equal parts beer and a form of lemonade, beer enthusiasts tend to recognize it by its more popular (and English) name—the shandy gaff.

Parting cup. Called a parting glass or stirrup cup in some regions, this was a drink consumed when saying good-bye, or for other occasions as appropriate. People partook of beer-based parting cups as a sign of friendship. It was a way of saying that parting was nearly too much to bear.

With those that drink before they dine—
With him that apes the grunting swine,
Who fills his page with low abuse,
And strives to act the gabbling goose
Turned out by fate to feed on grass—
'Boy, give me quick, the parting glass.'

The man, whose friendship is sincere,
Who knows no guilt, and feels no fear:—
It would require a heart of brass
With him to take the parting glass.

With him, who quaffs his pot of ale;
Who holds to all an even scale;
Who hates a knave, in each disguise,
And fears him not—whate'er his size—
With him, well pleased my days to pass,
May heaven forbid the PARTING GLASS.

(Philip Freneau)

To make your own parting glass, brown two pieces of toast and add to a quart of mild ale mixed with two-thirds of a bottle of sherry. Grate nutmeg into the mixture, then sweeten the ale mixture with simple syrup to taste, and immediately before serving pour in one bottle of soda water. See *stirrup cup* in this section.

Pop-in. More appropriately, pop-in could have been called pop-off, or pop-out—such was its strength. It was made by adding one quart of small beer to a quart of brandy. Just the thing to serve guests who unexpectedly "pop in."

Porter. Although this is a surprise to some, porter was originally a mixed drink that was most commonly referred to as entire. It comprised equal parts of ale, beer, and two penny. An alternate name when ordering was three thirds or three threads. The term *three threads* did not refer to threads on the tap (there were none) it was merely a vernacular expression for "thirds." The three thirds name came from the fact that the drink came from three separate kegs. In the early 1700s the ends (butts) of the kegs faced bar patrons, and they began calling porter a draw of entire butt, meaning it was from all three taps. See *porter* in the Beer and Beer Drinking section.

Porter gaff. As with the shandy gaff and the *panache,* this beer mixed drink uses lemonade in its formulation. Of course, in a porter gaff, the remaining half of the glass is filled with porter.

Posset. A mixed drink of the colonial period in America, posset was made with various types of alcohol serving as the base. All forms of posset used hot milk, heated until it curdled, as the base. In England's colonial period a favorite recipe called for the addition of warmed ale, sugar, ginger, and grated nutmeg. It was also known as ale posset.

Punch. Long known as a mixture of various fruit juices and liquors, at least one form of punch contained beer. To make a bowl of ale punch, combine ale, sherry, brandy, and spices. No measurements for any of the ingredients exist, you make it to your own particular taste.

Purl. In this drink warmed beer was fortified with gin and bitters. Some versions used spices, occasionally including Roman wormwood, gentian root, *Calamus aromaticus*, horseradish, dried orange peel, juniper berries, and seeds soaked in the beer. Heated, but only to a temperature at which a person could comfortably consume it at a single draft, it was popular in local areas of both England and colonial America. Purl was at times mixed and then allowed to mature for up to a year. It was also known as dog's nose.

Red eye. A commonplace mixture of tomato juice and beer. Also known as a ruddy Mary and as a red rooster.

Rider. Rider was the general term for any beverage that did not mix well with one previously consumed. An example would be following wine with beer.

Rosemary. During the sixteenth and seventeenth centuries this was one of the spices frequently used to flavor beer.

Ruddle. From southern England, this was a heated combination of hard liquor and beer with the addition of sugar and lemon peel. It is similar to hot pot, which was the name of choice in other locations.

Ruddy Mary. Related to red eye but spiced in the manner of a Bloody Mary, the base consists of beer and tomato juice.

Rum fustian. Odd as it sounds, this drink is misnamed, for it contains no rum. To prepare this beer-based drink . . .

> Separate the yolks of twelve eggs, beat them and add a quart of strong home-brewed beer, a bottle of white wine, half a pint of gin, a grated nutmeg, the juice from the peel of a lemon, a small quantity of cinnamon, and sugar sufficient to sweeten it.

In this preparation the beer was heated and the other ingredients were added to it.

Sack posset. Also known simply as posset. A favorite recipe of the day was prepared, as was any posset, by heating milk. In the following version, the person making it had to:

> Boil a quart of cream with quantum sufficit of sugar, mace, and nutmeg; take a half a pint of sack and the same quantity of ale, and boil them well together, adding sugar; these being boiled separately are now to be added. Heat a pewter dish very hot, and cover your basin with it, and let it stand by the fire for two or three hours.

As with a great number of mixed beer drinks posset was intended to be taken hot. A common belief of the 1600s was that drinking cold liquids was bad for health.

Scurvy grass ale. One of the many old curatives based on beer, this was an ale infused with watercress, and it claimed to ward off the dreaded disease scurvy.

> *But to conclude this drinking-aley-tale,*
> *We had a sort of ale called scurvy ale.*
>
> *(Taylor [1618])*

Sean O'Farrell. Faded from common application, this was once a slang term in the United States for a shot and a beer. See *boilermaker* and *depth charge* in this section.

Shandy gaff. A well-known beer mixed drink of England with variations found in nearly every spot on the globe. To make one, mix equal parts beer and lemonade (although what passes for British lemonade tastes more like soda). This drink's roots go back to the days when adding spices to beer was common. The original shandy was made of beer, ginger, and either ginger ale or ginger beer. By the 1800s the shandy had evolved into a form close to what bars serve today. A recipe from that period advised to start with a pint of beer and pour in one bottle of ginger beer.

Shot and a beer. As the name implies, a shot glass of hard liquor chased down with a beer. Very close to a boilermaker—only technique separates them.

Skip-and-go-naked. Mixed like a large punch, this drink contains beer, gin, lemon juice, and a splash of grenadine. The best renditions were reportedly mixed in a (it is hoped) clean garbage can.

Snakebite. Why would anyone order a snakebite? A rhetorical question that does not merit the least debate. A snakebite contains identical portions of beer and cider and works with the speed of a snake bite to put people into a deep coma.

Snow on Black Butte. Created by chef Ron Baker, and inspired by Sam Barbiere, this ranks as one of the best beer confections. Begin by layering chocolate mousse in the bottom of a glass to the depth of about three-quarters of an inch. On top of the mousse form a second layer of caramel sauce, followed by a third layer of raspberry sauce. With a bent spoon gently pour Deschutes Black Butte Porter over the layers, and top with two scoops of vanilla ice cream. See *apple Florentine* in this section.

Spices. Spices have been added to beer throughout its history. Recipes for old brews included spices to help preserve the beer and for flavoring. Often, when used for medicinal purposes the spices were thought to perform a specific function. For example, today many winter beers have an infusion of nutmeg:

> *And Notemuge to put in ale*
> *Whether it be moist or stale.*

> (Chaucer)

Other spices, too, were common:

> *Nutmegs and ginger, cinnamon and cloves,*
> *And they gave me this jolly red nose.*
>
> *(Beaumont and Fletcher)*

And spiced cakes were also floated in ale:

> *Will he will drinke, yet but a draught at most,*
> *That must be spiced with a nut-browne tost.*
>
> *(Wither)*

Think of the addition of spices as being as natural to beer as drinking it. Spiced beer was said to aid in the restoration of bodily powers. What better reason to lift a pint?

Steel bottom. It must have been devised as the Caribbean's answer to the boilermaker. In this case rum is substituted for whiskey and dropped into a glass of light lager.

Submarino. A variation of that barroom classic the depth charge, in this case a shot glass of tequila gets dropped into a glass of beer.

Syllabub. A milk-and-ale based drink that included other liquors as well, including wine, rum, brandy, and port along with a variety of spices. Served hot, it was popular in England toward the end of the 1700s. Also spelled cillabub or sillabub.

Tango. What the French call a beer cocktail. It is made of pale beer and grenadine. Sounds better than it tastes.

Teacher creature. Flavored with either Teacher's scotch or Teacher's Highland Cream, it forms an unlikely alliance by mixing Scottish ale and Drambuie®. Drinking too many may prevent you from watching the late Saturday night horror show of a similar name.

Teddy bear. A way to refer to the odd mixture of stout and port.

Tewahiddle. Known as a nightcap, this drink was made from a pint of table beer, a tablespoonful of brandy, and a teaspoonful of brown sugar or clarified syrup. A little grated nutmeg or ginger may have been added, and a roll of very thinly cut lemon peel. The preceding recipe was first recorded in London in 1654.

Three heads. A corruption of "three threads."

Three threads. In old England, the word *threads* was a local pronunciation of "thirds," and the drink called three threads was made by mixing equal portions of beer from three different casks. The beers used to make three threads were beer, ale, and two penny. Eventually a beer was brewed to duplicate the taste of three threads, and the name of that beer evolved into porter. See *porter* in the Beer and Beer Drinking section.

Tomboy. One of the names for a drink of mixed tomato juice and beer.

Turkish blood. Though it sounds exceptionally horrible, people actually made and drank this mixture of ale and Burgundy red wine. It makes you wonder once again about such beer and wine mixed drinks. Why ruin a perfectly good beer?

Twos. Regional English expression for a beer mixed drink made of mild and bitter. See *half and half* and *nuts and bolts* in this section.

Warm ale cup. Implied rightly in the name, a warm cup of ale or beer was once a common drink. Physicians believed warm liquids were easier to digest. To make a warm ale cup, start with one pint of ale, add a quarter pound of sugar, and bring to a boil. Next, add a second pint of ale together with one glass of brandy, two glasses of sherry, and spices to individual preference (spices used were traditionally nutmeg and cinnamon). It might not actually assist in digestion, but then again, you wouldn't care.

Weiss mit schuss. A refreshingly effervescent brew, Berliner *weisse* to some drinkers is too intense. For them, a shot of raspberry syrup mellows the nature of the beer. Germans mix another variation with woodruff, a syrup produced from the infusion of the herb that goes by that name.

Whistle-belly-vengeance. A most curious mixture, this was altogether the rage in Salem, Massachusetts, during colonial days. This little delight was probably born of New Englanders' well-known thrift. To begin, the tavern keeper soured a batch of household beer. From there the success of the venture turns even more dubious, for after the beer soured it was simmered in a kettle and sweetened with molasses. Finally, crumbs of "ryneinjun" bread were added for thickening, and the drink was served piping hot.

White ale. A mixture of ale prepared more for medicinal purposes than as a cocktail. A white ale included beer, rum, eggs, salt, and flour on its ingredient list. It seems the flour contributed to both the appearance and the name.

Winter ales. See *holiday beers* in this section.

Winter beers. See *holiday beers* in this section.

Winter warmers. See *holiday beers* in this section.

Wormwood. A bitter and aromatic shrub that was credited in medieval Europe with medicinal powers. An infusion in ales produced a drink popular in the 1600s.

Yard of flannel. The book titled *Cook's Oracle* provided the name yard of flannel as an alternative to flip, but these drinks from England in the 1600s are made from an identical recipe. Another source insisted that yard of flannel was slightly different. The ingredients included heated ale, brandy or rum, beer, brown sugar, ginger and other spices to taste, lemon peel, and beaten whole eggs.

Beer Bottles, Barrels, Glasses, Vessels, and Measures

uite a celebration must have taken place when our ancestors accidentally discovered beer. Their reaction to the delightful mistake of fermentation was probably an immediate attempt to brew another batch. Later, basking in the afterglow of a second successful brew, they turned their attention to bigger problems. Specifically, how to drink the stuff.

Imagine those early imbibers taking turns sticking their heads in a large clay pot for a swallow of beer. Strange as it may seem, their first solution for a more manageable way to drink beer was to use straws. In fact using a straw was better because they could insert it below the floating bits of grain on the surface and above the yeast settled on the bottom. The only problem was that it proved awful hard to take a big gulp, and face it, sometimes beer is most satisfying when quaffed.

Their solution was to make a beer mug. Whether of fired earthenware, carved wood, shaped leather, metal, or of the modern innovation, glass, the general cup or bowllike shape of a beer mug has been in use for millennia. It may have assumed many forms along the way, been called a variety of names, and held a wide range of beer styles, but people always used it for enjoying a good brew.

As the love of beer grew and evolved into an industry, brewers were faced with problems of storage and transportation. Their solution was the first beer keg.

With kegs and beer mugs available it seemed as though things could not be better; however, one difficulty did arise, when someone said, "Hey, I didn't get my fair share." That statement of dissatisfaction initiated the development of weights and measures. As time passed glasses, tumblers, kegs, casks, and barrels all assumed a standard shape and volume, but history and beer still managed to produce a few oddities along the way.

An ornate beer bowl used as an early drinking vessel.

Agrafe. Brewers use this device to secure a cork on a bottle. Consisting of a metal band that runs under one bottle lip, up across the cork, and down to the opposite bottle lip, it prevents the cork from escaping as pressure from carbonation builds up in a bottle. It was, in effect, the type of "bottle cap" used in the colonies during the 1400s and 1500s to seal bottles. To this day you may occasionally find agrafes on certain bottle-conditioned Belgian beers.

Ale barrel. A barrel or cask of English origin that contains thirty-two imperial gallons. Not to be confused with the similar beer barrel, which holds thirty-six gallons.

Ale-bowl. An early drinking vessel for ale from the 1400s and 1500s that was probably made of wood. During festivals and feasts it would be passed from one celebrant to another until drained. It was then refilled, and the process of joyously passing it about was repeated.

Ale glass. A stemmed glass with a long and narrow shape in which ale is served.

Ale horn. A crude drinking vessel made by hollowing out a large animal horn. Some are equipped with a wooden or metal stand. This creation is credited to the old Norse.

Ale jug. Another name for a beer jug. It's not a capped jug but a large glass. Dating from the 1700s, an ale jug was a large glass holding approximately one quart of beer.

Ale warmer. An essential English bar tool of the 1700s, when heated beer-based drinks were all the rage. It was made of brass or copper in a conical shape with a flat bottom. Placed above the coals, typically on a grate in the fireplace, it heated the ale. It was also called an ass's ear.

Aleyard. Also known as yard of ale. A tall slender glass with a funnel-shaped top and a bulb- or globe-shaped base that is used as a drinking vessel. One explanation of its origin holds that it was designed in this length and shape for ease in handing to the seated driver of a horse-drawn coach. Use of this glass requires a technique of twisting or swirling the bulb to gently slosh the beer down the flute and funnel-shaped portion, thereby avoiding a sudden gush of beer from the bottom of the glass.

Amber. Dating from the Dark Ages, this was a measure of about seven gallons. Records speak of King Ini of the West Saxons, who in 694 imposed what has been considered the first tax on English beers. It was a payment made in ale and measured in ambers. It could be thought of as a type of assessment based upon a farmer's acreage.

Amphora. An ancient Greek pottery jar, the *amphora* had two handles and a pointed end that was pushed into the ground to hold it upright. It was also a unit of measure equal, in the ancient Roman version, to about nine gallons. Think of it as the original firkin.

Ass's ear. The vessel English tavern keepers used to warm ale in the days when hot-ale drinks were popular, from the mid 1500s to the mid 1700s. See *ale warmer* in this section.

Baby. A small beer bottle with a capacity one-fourth the size of a normal bottle. In the time of its popularity during the 1800s it was equal to a gill (about one cup). Perhaps it received this name because it was so cute?

Baloon. The French word for what English speakers call a snifter. Designed with a large bowl that can be warmed by cupping the hands around it to allow aromatics to escape, these are then retained by the shape of the bowl. An excellent glass for use with a strong ale or barley wine.

Balthazar. Friends may be required to help carry this bottle. Fortunately, it holds a sufficient amount to go around. The biblical name applies to an oversized bottle. A balthazar contains the equivalent of sixteen standard-size wine bottles, which translates to a volume of about three gallons.

Baptism. During the 1200s in Europe some churches used beer to baptize babies instead of water. Letters of Pope Gregory to Archbishop Nidrosiensi of Iceland make mention of the practice.

Barrel. Long used as a conventional measure. The capacity varies according to the country, and whether it holds wet or dry contents. For beer the standard barrel holds 31.5 U.S. gallons. See *cask* in this section.

Barril. The Spanish and Portuguese word for barrel.

Barriquant. The French word for a small barrel or cask.

Tax collector measuring the volume of bottles.

Barrique. A French version of the hogshead, which contains approximately 50 gallons. The capacity of a *barrique* varies according to region—from a low of 45.5 gallons in the regions of Champagne, Cognac, and Burgundy to a high of 50 gallons in Anjou and Sauternes. The English also use the term, and English barriques contain about 50 gallons.

Beaker. It might sound like something out of a lab, but this is the English word for a beer glass. A beaker most closely resembles an extra large beer mug without the handle.

Beer barrel. A wooden cask slightly larger than an ale barrel and holding about 36 gallons.

Beer can. Aside from the more modern meaning, this originally was an alternate name for a large pail, growler, or jug in which the consumer carried beer home from the brewery or tavern.

Beer from (in) the wood. A phrase used in England and Germany to describe beer drawn directly from a wooden cask.

Beer jug. In the 1700s this was a large glass holding approximately one quart of beer. In more modern times it was synonymous with a growler— a vessel designed to carry fresh beer, purchased at a brewery or tavern, home for consumption.

Bellarmine. Also known as graybeard and longbeard. Named after a certain Cardinal Bellarmine, this drinking vessel was named by Dutch Protestants to mock the Catholic church. It was an oversized drinking jug made of stoneware with a large belly and a narrow neck.

Biblical bottles. Oversized bottles roughly based upon the volume and shape of a standard wine bottle but used for either beer or wine. The names of these bottles are taken from characters in biblical stories. The names and volumes follow, in ascending order:

Magnum	2 bottles
Jeroboam	4 bottles
Rehoboam	6 bottles
Methuselah	8 bottles
Salamanazar	12 bottles
Balthazar	16 bottles
Nebuchadnezzar	20 bottles

Black Jack. An old English and colonial American drinking vessel manufactured by forming leather over a mold and sealing it with tar or pitch. A quote from the Roxburghe Ballads refers to:

Black Jacks to every man
Were filled with wine and beer
No pewter Pot or Canne
In those days did appear.

Bock. In France this word may refer not only to a beer but also to a drinking vessel. Bocks have a shape similar to a large tankard made of glass.

Boggle. Scotland gave the world this unusual drinking tankard in an odd human shape. It was the size of a pitcher or jug and made of molded or shaped leather. Rather mind boggling.

Bombard. This large vessel dates to the Elizabethan era, when big pewter vessels were too heavy to lift or carry and inexpensive glass was not yet available. Drinkers naturally resorted to an older method of making drinking vessels by devising this oversized jug of molded leather sealed with pitch.

Boot. A vessel made of pewter, or glass. Large, and in the size and shape of a coachman's distinctive boot, boots were used to carry mulled ale out to the driver of a coach. Later, they were widely used by fraternities to initiate unsuspecting new members. Drinking from a boot the wrong way causes a flood of beer to wash over the victim's face. Many other designs of such trick glasses, such as a cocked hat, were also popular. To drink from a boot, simply turn the toe out to either side.

Botte. A large drinking glass from France with a volume of about one liter.

Bottle. See *leathern bottle* in this section.

Bottle cap. A simple metal device that bottlers press down over the mouth of a bottle, the overlapping metal grips the bottle and provides the seal. Also known as a crown cap or a crown cork.

Brage beaker. Norse in origin, this was a drinking vessel over which vows were made. It may also be called a bragging cup. Though the old Norse usually made good on their vows, whether they fortified them by drink or not.

Brown cow. A slightly outdated English slang term used to describe a cask of ale. It derived from ale's original color and was a euphemism for a beer cask (milk was, of course, a more acceptable drink, so beer drinkers employed this term to disguise the object of their affection).

Bumper. Any drinking vessel filled to the brim or the point of overflowing. The use of *bumper* reaches back to the practice of Catholics toasting *au bon Pere*—to the health of the good pope" after a feast. Repeating the French quickly reveals this word's origin. See *rasade* in this section.

Bung. The plug used to seal a bung-hole.

Bung-hole. Coopers bored a hole in the side of a barrel at its widest point (the middle) to create an opening for filling the cask with beer. When filled, a bung, or spline, sealed the hole.

Butt. A large cask, keg, or barrel of varying capacity but usually 108 gallons. Another common name was "pipe." A butt contained two hogsheads. It was also the term used for the flat, circular end pieces on each keg or barrel.

Canette. A type of beer mug with a cone or cylinder shape that was popular in sixteenth-century Germany and Switzerland, then later in England. It held a quart of liquid. The word is also an outdated French measure for beer equaling about 1 1/2 pints.

Cann. A drinking mug that stood upon a molded base and had either a single or double scrolled handle. It held one pint. Also spelled can.

Capsule. A lead, foil, or other soft-metal cover placed upon corked bottles. It was originally positioned over the end of the bottle to protect the cork from weevils, then later from dust. Now used more as a decorative cover, capsules are still found on many beer bottles.

Carboy. Any number of glass or earthen jugs or bottles of varying sizes used to hold beer and other liquids. Often these were protected by being encased in wood or wicker. The most common modern size holds five gallons.

Cask. A cylindrical wooden container that bulges around the middle. It is fabricated of curved and shaped wooden staves that run along the cask's axis and is held together by metal hoops. Later casks are made of drawn aluminum and stainless steel, which have largely replaced the difficult-to-maintain wooden casks. Although a barrel implies a specific capacity, a cask can be of varying size. Names of casks, their countries of origin, and their corresponding capacities follow:

Filling casks in the late Middle Ages.

Arroba	Spain	12 to 18 liters
Baril	Portugal	16.74 liters
Barile	Italy	58.34 liters
Barrique	France	200 to 248 liters
Botte	Sardinia	500 liters
Brente	Switzerland	50 liters
Dreiling	Austria	1,358 liters
Eimer	Switzerland	37.5 liters
Füder	Austria	824.42 liters
Ohm	Germany	128 to 150 liters
Oka	Balkans	1.28 liters
Piece	France	200 to 250 liters

Pipe	England	477 liters
Pipe	Portugal	502 liters
Pipe	Spain	416 liters
Stuck	Germany	1,200 liters
Vedro	Russia	12.39 liters

Caudle cup. A two-handled cup in which the hot gruel-based drink caudle was served.

Chime. Where the staves come together at the end of a barrel is called the chime. It is the circular rim at the end of the barrel that is formed by the staves, and it is where the head of the cask is set. Also spelled chimb, chine.

Ciderkin. Not to be confused with the other "kins" (barrels) this was actually an inferior cider made from the remains of the pressing.

Coaching glass. Much like a yard, this was a glass with no base that could not stand upright without support. It was designed for ease in handing up to the seated passengers and drivers of a coach, who would drink it in one draft.

Cocked hat. A humorous beer glass that leaks onto any drinker who does not know its secret.

Conigus. Of Roman origin this is a unit of liquid measure equal to about one-half gallon.

Conoid. A mathematical word to describe a barrel. Essentially, the barrel's shape consists of two cones with the pointed tops removed and attached base to base.

Contracting cup. A ceremonial drinking cup that dates to the Elizabethan era. It was used when a couple living far from a church, and unable to travel there, wished to enter into a contract of marriage. They would each drink from the cup in the presence of others and make a pledge to the other. The contract made in that fashion was considered binding, sort of a churchless wedding ceremony. Oh that life were still that simple.

Cooper. A person trained in the construction and repair of casks and barrels. Highly skilled coopers carve the staves of barrels individually. During industrialization, American manufacturers devised methods for machine-cutting barrels.

Cork. The original seal for beer bottles. When used alone, as they were centuries ago, corks require a wire cage or a "capsule" to aid in containing the pressure within the bottle.

Corkage. A fee charged by a bar or restaurant to those who bring their own bottles in to consume on the premises. In some places this also applies to any bottle bought within the establishment.

Crinze. Hybrid cross between a bowl or cup and a small tankard. Crinzes were made of earthenware.

Crown cap. Invented by William Painter in 1892, it revolutionized the way beer was sold. Crown cap was the original name for the first practical way to seal bottles. Made of thin metal with a cork backing that prevented the beer from contacting the metal, its lightweight, cheap construction and firm seal opened the take-home market to breweries. Also known as a crown cork.

Cuarto. A Spanish liquid measure equaling a quarter of a cask.

Cullet. Used mainly in association with bottling lines, it describes the accumulation of broken glass. Brewers do not throw away the cullet, which can be recycled. New meltings always use a little cullet as a "seed" for the new batch of glass.

Cup. Springing from the same root was the style of cup that looks like a goblet and the type used for hot beverages. The name is derived from the Latin *cupa*, and the shape of the bowl resembles a cask. See *cupa* in this section.

Cupa. Latin word to describe a vat, barrel, or cask. It is the origin of the words cup, goblet, and cooper.

An ornate version of a drinking cup, which was the forerunner to a beer mug.

Cuve. A French word describing any vat used in association with fermented beverages. Type and size do not matter, nor does the material of construction. The *cuve* can be made of wood, metal (glass-lined or enameled), earthenware, cement, or stone. The style comprises nearly all imaginable fermentation vats.

Cyathus. With ancient Roman origins, this is a dipper holding about 1 1/3 fluid ounces.

Decant. A technique used when pouring liquid from bottles that contain a layer of sediment. It describes the process of pouring from the bottle slowly and with care to draw off the clear liquid while leaving the sediment behind.

Deckelpokal. Of German origin, the word describes a type of covered stein usually made of metal.

Demi. A French beer glass that originally held approximately a pint. In modern application it has a capacity of about ten ounces.

Demi-firkin. A small beer barrel with a liquid capacity of approximately 4 1/2 gallons. Also known as a pin. See *pin* in this section.

Demijohn. A jar or jug of between one and ten gallons capacity, made of glass or earthenware. *Demijohns* are encased in a form-fitting woven wicker basket with a handle. Of French origin, the name may have originated in the town of Damagan with corruption of the town's name leading to "demijohn."

Demion or demis-setier. An outdated French measure that equaled a little less than a half cup.

Dip rod. A stick with graduated measurements used to determine the volume of liquid in a barrel. With the dip rod inserted at an angle, an experienced person can correctly identify the amount of liquid in the barrel.

Dock glass. A glass used by English excise officers stationed at the docks. It held five ounces, one-quarter of an imperial pint.

Dolium. An oversized earthen jar of the ancient Romans. It was an extralarge version of an *amphora.*

Drinking horn. Various peoples have hollowed out animal horns to use as drinking vessels, among them the ancient Greeks and the old Norse. Often the horn's builder would attach it to a stand that held it upright when it was set down.

Dry inches. Outdated now, this was a term used by excise officials to indicate the amount of ullage (empty space above the liquid) in a cask.

Fass. The German word for cask or barrel. The old Austrian *fass* held approximately 125 imperial gallons.

Fässchen. The German word for any small cask or keg.

Fassweise. It could be mistaken as a designation for a kegged weisse beer, but it is actually the German word for "on draft" from the barrel. It is more closely tied to wine than to beer.

Feuillette. A designation for casks half the size of a French barrique, which varied in volume from region to region. Therefore, a *feuillette* held anywhere between 100 and 115 gallons.

Firing glass. Said to have its roots in the Freemasons, this is a drinking vessel that is constructed with an extrastrong base, and with good reason. When acknowledging a toast or other salutation, the glasses are slammed in unison on a table, creating a report likened to the firing of a gun.

Firkin. Casks (barrels) that hold nine imperial gallons were once quite common in England, and the name for one was firkin. In capacity it straddled the size between modern quarter and half barrels. Two firkins equaled one kilderkin, and a barrel half the size of a firkin was called a pin.

Flagon. A cylindrical drinking vessel that tapers in toward the top. Somewhat similar to a modern tankard or mug, flagons were originally fitted with a lid and in the Middle Ages were reserved for use in religious ceremonies.

> *St. George he was for England,*
> *and before he killed the dragon.*
> *He drank a pint of English ale*
> *Out of an English flagon.*
>
> (G. K. Chesterton)

Later, flagons became a common drinking vessel and eventually were called tankards. In more modern times, flagon is the name for a beer bottle of two-quart capacity in Australia.

Flask. In modern times, *flask* brings to mind a small flat bottle made of metal and contoured to fit concealed in a pocket. In its original version it was a long-necked bottle with a bulbous body.

Flogger. In the days when bottles were corked, the hammer used to drive the cork into the bottle was called a flogger.

F-measure. A quantity defined in London of the 1300s as the standard amount of beer sold for a farthing.

Foot bath. An infrequently used name for a large glass of beer.

Formidable. In France, the name for an exaggerated beer glass with a capacity of over three liters. It's also known as a baron. In Belgium, a formidable holds a more modest volume of one liter.

Frog mug. One of the many glasses, tankards, mugs, and other drinking vessels designed as a practical joke. It is constructed so that as a person drains its contents they will discover a realistic-looking frog attached to the bottom.

Fuddling-cup. A very elaborately contrived drinking vessel made with a series of interconnecting passages. Unwitting victims cannot escape a dousing, and only those with knowledge of its design escape dry.

Fuder. An oversized German storage cask that holds up to four hundred gallons.

Gallon. In the United States this unit of measure equals 128 fluid ounces. The U.S. gallon equals only 5/6 of the larger imperial gallon used as a standard measure in the United Kingdom.

Gill. A unit of measure close to one-half cup in size (about four ounces). Also the name for a ground ivy used in older days (before the time of hops) to stabilize and preserve beer.

Gispen. Constructed in a similar manner as a jack, the gispen was a small mug-shaped container made of leather and holding five to ten ounces of beer. Used in England in the sixteenth and seventeenth centuries, gispens were less popular than the much larger of jacks. Another version, called the gaspin, was sized between a black jack and a bombard. Other spellings include gyspen, gyspyn, gaspin, and gespin.

Glasses. Beer glasses have not always been made of glass. Fashioned from a variety of materials they can be constructed of: wood, clay, leather, pewter, silver, horn, ostrich eggs, skulls, shells, gourds, and more. The names are even more diverse. Among the names used throughout history are cup, bowl, tankard, pin, tumbler, mug, can, bombard, greybeard, yard, long-glass, hanap, stein, jack, bottle, goblet, jug, baloon, beaker, jar, jorum, bellarmine, boggle, boot, bumper, canette, cocked hat, crinze, formidable, and gispen.

Glassware. Before the mid-1800s a drinking vessel made of glass was rare. In part this was because glass itself was rare, and why produce a tankard of expensive glass that some oaf might break during a beer bust? Before glassware beer was a dark, unattractive, and rather murky beverage, but the development of pale beers, which coincided with advances in glassmaking, brought about a revolution in beer drinking. Suddenly it was not only fun to drink beer, it was also visually appealing, and people rushed to fill their new glass mugs with beer. As competition increased, specialized designs were introduced. Flutes, bowls, tulips, and thistles all lent their familiar figures to glasses, each highlighting the most notable attribute of the beers they were designed to hold. Flutes released the effervescence of Pilseners. Bowls warmed and enhanced the complexities of barley wine. Tulips spilled the head and ale equally in strong Belgian ales. Thistles trapped the aromatics of beers, as with the faint smoky maltiness of Scotch ale.

Goblet. A large bowl sitting upon a short stem, in its original form it looked similar to a chalice, or a drinking cup without handles. The name was derived from the Latin *cupa,* meaning cask, and the shape of the bowl resembles a half-cask. Typically, a goblet holds nine to twelve ounces.

God-forgive-me. Old English taverns had a number of bartending tools sitting near the hearth because hot beer drinks were a popular libation. Nearly every bar had a god-forgive-me or its equivalent. This was a tall stone mug or jug with two handles that was filled with beer and then set in the coals and ashes to warm. When the beer began steaming it was ready to begin mixing for cocktails.

Grace cup. A beer-drinking vessel used by monks for giving thanks to the Lord for yet another day of beery refreshment and nourishment. It was also a cup used to drink the beer-based mixed drink called a grace cup. See *grace cup* in the Beer-Based Mixed Drinks section.

Greybeard. A Dutch drinking mug that was also used in England. It was shaped to resemble Cardinal Bellarmine, who wore a square-cut grey beard. It was squat with a narrow neck, which mimicked the cardinal's physique. See *Bellarmine* in this section.

Growler. In the days before the handy take-home six-pack, a growler was the way to get beer home. Originally constructed as a metal pail with a lid, the consumer would have it filled at the local brewery or tavern. The modern version has assumed the form of a glass jug.

Gyngleboy. A decorative jack (leather drinking vessel) that gained favor in England of the 1500s. Gilded and adorned with ornamental patterns and often small silver bells, it was used as a bar game or challenge—to see if the drinker could consume the entire gyngle without making it jingle.

Halfpiece of wood. An English term describing a liquid measure of ale. It dates from the 1400s.

Hamster. In some regions of the United States this was a name for partially consumed bottles of beer forgotten or left behind by their owners. In some circles a beer left behind even momentarily was declared a hamster and considered fair game. See *old trousers* in the Beer-Based Mixed Drinks section.

Hanap. A ceremonial English drinking vessel from the 1500s and 1600s that was made of pewter. Hanaps were tall and shaped much like a goblet. They were stored in a "hanaper," a type of woven wicker basket. The basket's name remains with us to this day—from it was derived the word *hamper*.

Head. In a barrel or cask, the head is a flat circular wooden piece at each end. Also called a butt.

Head space. What do you call nothing, or at least the space that nothing occupies? Head space is the word for the volume of any vessel not filled with beer. In other words, the empty side of the half-full question. See *ullage* in this section.

Hectoliter. A unit of liquid measure in use throughout the metric-oriented world. It is equal in capacity to 26.4 U.S. gallons (22 imperial gallons). One hundred liters (a liter bit more than a quart) make up a hectoliter.

Heeltap. The name applied to any liquid left at the bottom of a glass.

Hefeweizen glasses. Designed to hold precisely the contents of a seventeen-ounce hefeweizen bottle, the shape also accentuates both the head and aroma of the famous German wheat beers. Accomplished wheat-beer drinkers enjoy pouring the beer by quickly inverting the bottle and drawing it up at a rate that keeps the bottle's lip fully immersed in the head but barely beneath the level of the rising beer. If performed properly, this results in an empty bottle in one hand and a full glass of hefeweizen with no overflowing beer in the other. When toasting with a hefeweizen glass, tap bottoms together (they were designed to take such stress) but avoid the thin glass at the top.

Hogarth glass. A glass named to honor William Hogarth, who portrayed this type of squat, wide-based vessel in his art.

Hogshead. A large keg about twice the size of a standard beer barrel with a capacity of between 54 and 140 gallons. In England the hogshead measures 54 gallons; a U.S. hogshead has a volume equal to 2 standard barrels, or about 63 gallons. And then there's the name—a beer drinker's barrel if there ever was one.

Hollowing bottle. In Hampshire, in England, between the 1500s and 1600s, farmers would celebrate the end of the harvest by sending to the field a large bottle containing nearly ten gallons of strong beer. As the beer was poured around, the head carter would sing:

> *Well ploughed—well sowed,*
> *Well reaped—well mowed,*
> *Well aried, and*
> *Never a load overthro'd*

When finished with the song he would raise his hand, a signal for all to cheer. The little ritual was called the hollowing bottle.

Hoop. An alternate name for the bands used to hold together a barrel, keg, or cask.

Hopir. A liquid measure used in England during the fifteenth century.

Horn. Before the introduction of glass, many materials were adopted for use in constructing beer drinking vessels. Animal horns were one. They were hollowed out and used to hold beer in the way a cup was used. Often the owner would decorate the horn with drawings, carvings, and rich inlays of precious metal.

Hum glass. Actually a small tumbler, a hum glass was filled with a heated mix of beer and ale. See *hum* in the Beer-Based Mixed Drinks section.

Imperiale. A bottle of French origin, it was oversized and held between six to eight regular bottles.

Imperial gallon. Equal in volume to 160 fluid ounces this was a standardized British unit based on the volume filled by 10 pounds of water at 17 °C.

Jack. A mug formed of leather and sealed with pitch to hold liquids, commonly beer. Because of its color it was also called black jack. See *black jack* and *bombard* in this section.

Jar. Traditionally cylindrical earthenware container of England dating from the 1500s and 1600s. In larger sizes, up to ten gallons, jars were used for storing liquids. In smaller sizes they served as drinking vessels.

Jeroboam. A large bottle for holding either beer or wine. It has a capacity now standardized as equal to four normal bottles, although at one time some jeroboams held as many as eight to twelve. See *biblical bottles* in this section.

Jordan. A name no longer used for any long-necked bottle.

Jorum. A pewter drinking mug that held one-half pint.

Jug. A large-volume vessel designed more for storing liquid than drinking, although some people would not be adverse to an occasional pull on a jug. It had a handle for ease in carrying.

Jungfrauenbecher. A German drinking cup used at weddings. It has the shape of a woman in a billowing dress who holds a basket over her head. When the cup is turned over, the dress acts as a large glass, and the pivoting basket can also be filled. The groom must drink carefully from the dress shape without spilling the contents of the basket, which he passes on to his bride.

Keg. Nowadays people use "barrel" and "keg" almost interchangeably. A keg used to be almost any small barrel with a volume of less than ten gallons. In modern usage, "pony keg" refers to the smaller-sized barrel.

Kilderkin. Close to the volume of the modern (half) barrel found in most draft beer accounts, the kilderkin was of a size equal to eighteen imperial gallons. A cask half the size of a kilderkin was the firkin (nine imperial gallons).

Knitting cup. Elizabethan-era weddings observed a tradition of acknowledging the marriage by passing around a communal cup. Lavishly decorated and designed with three handles, each person at the wedding drank from the knitting cup immediately following the ceremony.

Kylix. Originating in Roman-occupied England, the kylix was a shallow drinking cup mounted on a long stem. Made either of bronze or silver, it was known as a tazza in Elizabethan England.

Lady's waist. Australian and Irish name for a glass holding one-half ounce. Perhaps exhibiting the self-control to limit yourself to only one of these would ensure the maintenance of a lady's waist.

Last drop glass. A glass so called because of the humorous figure etched into the inside bottom. The etching depicted a corpse hung on a gibbet. Thus, the last drop was the condemned criminal pictured hanging from the gallows, and the last drop always remained in the bottom of the glass.

Leaguer. An old Dutch term for a large cask or barrel with a capacity in excess of 153 U.S. gallons.

Leathern bottle. Early bottles were made of leather. Fashioned in the same manner as a black jack, the bottles had a neck fitted with a stopper. In this configuration bottles were used not only as drinking vessels (like the jack) but also as devices to carry beer.

> *A leather bottle we know is good,*
> *Far better than glasses or cans of wood;*
> *For when a man's at work in the field,*
> *Your glasses and pots no comfort will yield;*
> *But a good leather bottle standing by*
> *Will raise his spirits whenever he's dry.*
>
> *(Thomas Heywood [1635])*

In fact, most leather bottles were designed to hang at the side of farmers, pilgrims, travelers, and other people on the move.

Lion. A French drinking glass holding 40 centiliters. It equals .40 of a liter, which translates to a little more than 12 ounces.

Liter. A metric liquid measure based upon the volume occupied by 1 kilogram (weight equal to about 2.2 pounds) of water at 4 °C and an atmospheric pressure of 76 centimeters (mercury). Most of the world has adopted the metric system because, as a system based on units of tens, it greatly simplifies calculations.

Longbeard. One of the alternate names for the drinking tankard also called a greybeard or a Bellarmine.

Long glass. Some English taverns and colleges (particularly Eton College) preferred the name "long glass," as opposed to "yard," but both are trick glasses built with a bulb-shaped bottom and a long flute or trumpet rising up to a total length of a yard. Drinkers had to know the trick to using such a glass. It was considered great sport to treat an unknowing, uninitiated, and unsuspecting victim to a long glass full of beer. As the person approached the last of the beer a quick torrent would rush down the flute to flood the person's face in beer.

Long pull. The term comes from the time when beer engines (hand pumps) were used to draw beer from a cask. The barkeep had to pull the handle on the pump to draw a beer, and a "long pull" meant an extra full serving.

Loving cup. Large drinking vessels from the 1600s passed among friends were first called loving cups. Initially they could have been of any shape—it was the sharing of drink among friends that made it a "loving cup." Only in later years would it assume a chalicelike form.

Lug. Extending straight out from the sides of pitchers and some glasses, this is a handle to be used when pouring from the container.

Maas. In Alsace, in France, the *maas* was a local unit of measure equal to a little more than 1.6 liters, or approximately 53 ounces.

Magnum. An extralarge capacity bottle that at one time held two quarts. It was standardized at a capacity equal to two regular bottles.

Mazer. Most closely associated with mead, mazers were originally used as drinking vessels for any type of beverage. In fact, beer may have been the first drink to be consumed from a mazer. Made of wood and roughly in the shape of a bowl, the name mazer comes from a Middle English word for maple, the preferred wood for making one.

An old version of a standing mazer.

Mether. Ireland is home to the mether, a square version of the mazer. A mether is a wooden drinking cup with four handles. Accounts of the mether imply that it was mainly used for the consumption of mead. However, in a time when drinking vessels were in short supply it seems likely it would have served double duty if a cask of ale were tapped.

Methuselah. One of a series of outsized bottles, the methuselah honors the long-lived man in the Bible. It has a capacity equal to eight normal-sized wine bottles and when popped open makes quite a party.

Middy. A regional name used in Australia for a glass that holds one-half pint of beer.

Miserable. A French liquid measure equaling about one fluid ounce. Such a wee dram is indeed miserable.

Modius. A unit of measure with ancient Roman roots. No one seems to agree on the capacity, though. Most frequently it is cited to be about the equivalent to an English peck. In the 1400s it was again a unit of measure, and even that volume is in dispute.

Mug. Do you really need a description? A drinking vessel made from wood, leather (originally), clay, glass, pewter, and other metals and with a wide, cylindrical shape, large open mouth, and a rimmed base. Some were made without the hefty handle that most mugs have today.

Muid. Casks from France with a capacity of approximately sixty gallons are known as *muids.*

Muller. Though *muller* refers to a sturdy, large drinking vessel, it is more appropriately used to describe any large-volume container constructed for the preparation, and sometimes direct consumption, of mulled drinks.

Mullet. Also known as ale mullet. Funnel-shaped and made of copper, mullets were used as mullers for heating beer in a fire for the purpose of preparing beer-based mixed drinks.

Mutchkin. Scottish in origin, this word describes a unit of fluid measure equal to about 14.5 ounces.

Nebuchadnezzar. A bottle of such a size that you must gather friends and relatives and rent a pickup truck. If you intend to drink a nebuchadnezzar, you'll need all the help you can get. As with other oversized bottles, it receives its name from larger-than-life biblical characters and holds the equivalent of twenty standard bottles. Drinking a nebuchadnezzar presents no small challenge.

Neck. The part of a bottle that narrows just above the "shoulders" and that leads upward to the mouth, where the crown or cap attaches.

Nip. Originally an English bottle holding approximately ten ounces. In the United States it became a bottle measuring seven ounces but often refers to any bottle of around half the volume of a standard (U.S.) twelve-ounce bottle. It is also an obsolete term once used for ordering a half-pint of ale.

Noggin. Diminutive drinking vessel that holds about one-quarter of an English pint (about five ounces).

Octave. Based on the Latin word for eight, an *octave* was a cask or barrel that had a reputed capacity one-eighth as large as a pipe (a pipe was a barrel that contained 100 gallons or more). By that definition, an octave should have held about 12 1/2 gallons, but there have been mentions of octaves with a capacity of up to 18 gallons.

Ounce (fluid). Equivalent in volume to the space occupied by one ounce (weight) of water at 62 °F at standard atmospheric pressure (thirty inches of mercury).

Oxhorn cup. A name for a drinking vessel made from the horn of an ox. See *horn* in this section.

Parfait. A French beer glass holding one liter (slightly more than one quart).

Party ball, party barrel. Party ball in the United States and party barrel in the United Kingdom (after the shapes used in each country). These forms of draft-beer containers were designed to hold between 1.5 and 5 gallons, an amount sufficient for a small private party.

Peg. An early synonym for a small measure. It originated from the rationing imposed by a peg tankard. See *peg tankard* and *pins/pin tankard* in this section.

Peg tankard. A type of wooden drinking mug from the 1600s in England in which a row of pegs were fitted at uniform intervals down the inside. Usually six pegs divided two quarts of ale into eight sections of about one-half pint per section. One theory on the origin of the design speculates that the peg mug was introduced in reaction to a law declared by King Edward in the late 900s. Its purpose was to discourage heavy drinking. In that period drinking vessels represented a considerable investment for an alehouse, therefore, drinking was usually from a communal mug. The restrictions imposed by King Edward's law demanded punishment if a person drank beyond his peg. This practice also gave birth to the term "take him down a peg." Peg tankards were also commonly called pin tankards. A variation used hoops pressed into the tankards' inner surface to mark the levels.

Penny pot. When a quart of the best English ale fetched one penny in the 1600s, the vessel holding that amount was called a penny pot. That same container filled with small beer cost only one-half penny.

Pewter. Although it was first discovered by the ancient Romans, the use of pewter was not widespread until the late Middle Ages. A metal alloy of tin, lead, and other metals, it revolutionized beer-drinking vessels. Originally an inexpensive replacement for silver, it rapidly found a welcome role in taverns and inns. As people learned it retained no off-flavors, as wood and leather did, they happily switched to pewter tankards. See *tankard* in this section.

Piece. From Burgundy in the 1600s came this large wooden barrel, reportedly capable of holding the equivalent of between 200 and nearly 300 liters.

Piggin. Also called a pigg. An outdated but once fairly common term for a drinking mug. When introduced in the medieval period, this mug of about one pint capacity was made of pigskin, as were jacks. In later days it was produced from earthenware or metals. The pig and whistle often seen on English tavern signs is a corruption of "Piggen wassail," or the Christmas holiday celebrated with mugs of cheer.

Pilsener glass. Shaped like a steep inverted cone with a short stem leading directly to the base, the Pilsener glass was designed to quickly release the beer's effervescence while providing the most attractive display of Pilsener's bright, clean appearance.

Pin. A small cask holding a mere 4.5 imperial gallons (about 5.3 U.S. gallons). It holds half the volume of a firkin and one-fourth the capacity of a kilderkin.

Pins/pin tankard. In addition to a designation for a cask, "pin" was also a name used interchangeably with "peg," as in peg tankard and drinking to pegs. In some areas the phrase "drinking to pins" was common. A variation used hoops. See *peg tankard* in this section.

Pint. A volume of liquid measure that varies slightly from country to country. In England pints served in a pub holds the equivalent of 20 ounces (1/8 imperial gallon). In the United States the volume of a pint equals 1/8 gallon, or 16 fluid ounces.

Pinte. An old French measure roughly equal to the capacity of one U.S. quart.

Pipe. An oversized wooden barrel capable of holding one hundred gallons or more.

Pipkin. An earthenware bowl-shaped drinking vessel also known as a pot, as in "having a pot of ale." See *pot* in this section.

Pitch. Composed of coal tar, pitch was used by brewers, who applied this sticky, water repellent tarlike material as a coating for the insides of beer barrels. This protected both the beer and wood.

Pitcher. A large jug or container made with an open mouth and fashioned with a lip for pouring. Pitchers were made successively from leather, wood, earthenware, metal, and glass. Most likely the name came from the early leather versions. Leather was an inexpensive material for fashioning liquid containers but required waterproofing, pitch was the material used to seal the insides of the leather "pitchers."

Early pitchers were made of a variety of materials including earthenware.

Plimsoll line. Beer glasses throughout the world use a small line, usually etched about three-quarters of an inch below the rim, as a level indicator of a full measure. In England that marking is called the Plimsoll line. Originally it was the name for the load line on a cargo ship honoring Samuel Plimsoll, the British shipping reformer.

Poculum. An ancient Roman drinking cup. See *cyathus* in this section.

Pony. A smallish volume of measure, equivalent to 4 or 5 ounces, depending on the locality of England or Australia. In England it was started during the 1800s, when landlords would divide pints into five helpings for the saloon customers and four for the public bar customers, charging the same for each helping. In the United States the term may refer to either a small bottle of about 7 ounces or a keg that holds one-fourth that of a full U.S. barrel, approximately 7 1/4 gallons. As a liquid measure it was at one time equivalent to 1 fluid ounce.

Posset-pot. Heated beer mixed with warm curdled milk was once considered a remedy. Two-handled pots specially designed for making posset were called posset-pots. See *posset* in the Beer-Based Mixed Drinks section.

Posson. A French measure equaling approximately two fluid ounces.

Pot. Old English name for a drinking vessel. It was often made of earthenware. When drinkers called for a pot, the alehouse keeper would respond with a large foaming bowl or pot-shaped container of ale. Frequently these were used for communal drinking and happily passed among a roomful of merrymakers. *Pot* has survived in more modern usage in areas of Australia, where it describes beer glasses of various sizes. In some countries the pot was also a unit of measure. In Scandinavia it was approximately 1 3/4 pints, in Switzerland it equaled 2 3/4 pints, and in Belgium it was much larger, equaling a half liter. But in Portugal the measure spelled *pote* was largest. There it held about 1 gallon.

Pot crown. Weddings always seem to have had the most curious, and fun, customs. At one time a reception called for a bride to place a pot crown of ale (a drinking vessel similar to a fuddling cup) atop her head. Her admirers would then come forward to drink from it in turn.

Pottle. Also spelled potell. Encountered often in old English and early American writing, this was a unit of liquid measure equal to about one-half gallon. Its origin dates back to the 1400s.

Pounder. A name of affection for the classic English pint glasses.

Puncheon. Serious beer drinkers would favor these old wooden casks. Sized for a considerable thirst, they held about 72 gallons of beer. No doubt it was enough to make one punchy. From the 1200s to the 1800s casks were produced in a greater variety of sizes than in recent years. The English puncheon was one of the odd sizes of old. It had a capacity of 72 imperial gallons of beer. Other puncheons had a variety of sizes, ranging from 114 imperial gallons for rum to 120 imperial gallons for whiskey. In those days each individual brewery or distillery had its own coopers, and although standardization was eventually reached among the manufacturers of a competitive product, diversity remained.

Punt. The indentation on the bottom of a bottle. The punt was a deliberate design feature from the late 1600s that added strength to bottles holding liquid under pressure—most regularly carbonated beverages.

Purchase. On a tankard or mug, the purchase is the small piece on the top of the handle on which the drinker places his thumb to steady the glass and ease its lifting.

Puzzle jug. A trick glass designed so a user could only drink from it in one specific way. If the method wasn't followed the user earned a face, or front, full of beer. Also known as a wager jug.

Quaich. An ornate silver two-handled drinking bowl made in Scotland. *Quaich* now traditionally implies the drinking of Scotch whiskey. Earlier versions of the quaich were made to nearly any size and used for all types of beverages.

Quart. A liquid measure equal to thirty-two ounces in the U.S. quart and forty ounces in the imperial quart. The U.S. quart contains slightly less than a liter, and the imperial quart holds slightly more.

Quarte. In France, this is an old measure of volume equal to forty-six cubic inches.

Quarter cask. A barrel one-quarter the size of a pipe (a pipe holds about 100 gallons). The quarter cask runs between 25 and 35 imperial gallons.

Quartern. Generally speaking, not a unit of measure but a term to indicate one-fourth of any of a variety of liquid measures. The British have a now-obsolete unit with an identical name that measured 5 1/3 of a standard English bottle.

Rabbit. No longer in use, the term "rabbit" was once used to describe a wooden drinking vessel.

Raisonable. Don't dismiss all French beer glasses. This one had a respectable capacity of one liter.

Rasade. The French equivalent of saying *bumper*—the word indicating a glass or tumbler filled to the brim.

Rehoboam. An oversized bottle that is larger than a jeroboam (equaling the capacity of four bottles) but smaller than a methuselah (eight bottles). The rehoboam holds as much as six standard bottles.

Reputed pint. A measure of capacity equaling to 1/12 of an imperial gallon (about 13 ounces). In Australia, a reputed pint is a glass that contains 15 liquid ounces.

Reputed quart. A liquid measure with a capacity totaling just under 27 ounces—1/6 of an imperial gallon.

Roquille. An old French unit of measure equaling one-half of an ounce.

Round. A large wooden tun. Tuns resemble a half barrel mounted in a vertical position, but with straight rather than curved staves. Of three hundred gallons capacity, rounds acquired their name in the 1700s.

Sakazuki. Small china or lacquered sake drinking cups.

Sakazuki-Goto. Ceremonial way of making promises over a drink of sake.

Salamanzar. Another of the biblical bottles, this has a volume of serious proportions: It equals a dozen standard-sized bottles.

Schenelle. An earthenware drinking glass with a tall and slender shape and a cover.

Schooner. The actual shape may vary slightly, but generally a schooner is a tall, somewhat tapered beer glass with a fifteen-ounce capacity.

Schwenker. A large goblet-shaped glass with thin walls, also called a *baloon.* The thin glass forming the bowl allows the warmth of the drinker's hands to release aromatics from the liquid. Primarily used for brandy, schwenkers also serve well for holding barley wines and old ales.

Screw cap. A threaded cap designed to hold the pressure of carbonation within a bottle but that allows unsealing without the aid of a mechanical opener. A counterclockwise twist breaks the perforated metal band that snugly grips the lip molded as part of the bottle's neck.

Sediments. A common name for the material found in beer that layers on the bottoms of fermenters, conditioning tanks, casks, kegs, and bottles. The layer forms as suspended solids fall from the beer. Sediment appears with regularity at the bottom of hefeweizen bottles.

Seidel. A German drinking vessel in the same general family as a mug or tankard. It holds a bit more than one pint.

Serieux. How unfair to dismiss the French when speaking of beer culture. They invented the *serieux,* a large beer glass with room for more than two quarts of beer. Seems serious enough.

Sester. Both a unit of measure and a tax, this was an excise charged on a measure of sixteen gallons of beer. It was a practice followed in Great Britain.

Shive. Also called a spile. The shape resembles a piece of small tubing or a straw. The cellarman inserts one in the soft part of a plug (bung) in the side of a cask, thereby venting pressure from the keg. The shive helps control the amount of pressure, and resulting carbonation, in a cask of real ale. When the proper amount of pressure has been reached, a small plug is inserted in the shive to halt the venting. The process of venting and plugging requires a special skill highly valued by publicans.

Shoulders. That area on a bottle in which the wide cylindrical part, which holds the bulk of the volume, narrows to form the neck. Often the bottle shape somewhat resembles a human torso.

Sir John. Black jacks of greater than normal size went by the name Sir John in the Middle Ages.

Skirt. The wavy ridge that looks almost corrugated on the edge of a bottle cap (crown cap or crown cork). It grips the bottle and holds the cap firmly down on the bottle, providing a pressure-tight seal.

Soma. A unit of measure of Italian origin and equal to approximately twenty-two gallons.

Spigot. Also called a tap. Originally made of wood, the spigot is a device that allows a controlled means of drawing beer from a keg or cask. The old method of installing one called for a hammer to quickly and forcefully knock it through, replacing a plug installed in the butt of the keg. Spigots and taps come equipped with a type of valve called a petcock, a quick-operating valve built to allow a full flow of beer with only one-quarter turn on the handle.

Spile. An alternate name for the shive inserted into casks. See *shive* in this section.

Split. Any small bottle half the size of a normal one. Typically, for beer it would measure six to nine ounces. Also called nips, ponies, shorties, and stubbies by various breweries.

Stand of ale. A large barrel. The name has dropped from standard use.

Stave. Wooden barrels are made by skilled coopers whose most difficult task is the shaping of the long curved pieces called staves. Staves are held in place with metal bands, and their tight custom fit renders the barrel waterproof. Wood finishing of beer marries the flavors in a unique smoothness absent from beers finished in other kegs.

For all the benefits of wood casks, they have been largely replaced because they are extremely labor-intensive. As seasons change the wood expands and contracts, causing the cooper to substitute a smaller stave for one of the larger ones in the summer, a process that is reversed in the winter. The changing of staves forces breweries to build and maintain twice the number of wooden barrels than barrels made of modern materials.

Stein. Needs no explanation to most beer drinkers. Think of the stein as the German version of the English tankard. Usually found with lids, some steins have an open top. The name comes from the practice of constructing them from earthenware which has a stony hardness.

Steinie. A French bottle of one liter capacity that is used to hold all types of liquids, including beer.

Stillion. A wooden cradle used to hold kegs on their sides for tapping.

Stirrup cup. Not a drinking vessel but rather the last or parting cup after a convivial session of drinking. It derives from the practice of giving a guest one last drink as he was in the saddle (and stirrups) of his horse and ready to head home. Also known as a parting cup.

One for the road—in a stirrup cup.

Stoup. Also spelled stope. A drinking vessel from the Elizabethan era that ranged in capacity from one pint to nearly half a gallon. It also meant a large drink.

Stubbie. A small bottle with a capacity about half the size of a normal bottle.

Studebaker. A tankard of extraordinary size, it was inspired by a German pirate named Studebaker who was known for his unquenchable thirst. One of his habits was to invert his tankard after he drained it. His intent was to issue a challenge, as in a drinking contest.

Tankard. A large, squat mug-shaped English drinking glass of considerable volume, usually at least one reputed pint. On most examples the tankard had a fixed handle and occasionally two. Two handles were necessary because of the tankard's original size, slightly over three gallons. Individual models at times sported a hinged lid fixed to the top of the handle.

A working stiff's pleasure— a tankard of ale.

Tanzeman. A carved wooden drinking vessel of Swiss origin similar to the German buttenman.

Tappit hen. A tankardlike vessel holding more than two pints from which hot drinks were served. An attached cover kept the beverages warm, and the vessel received its name from the shape of the lid, which looked like the crest of a hen. As the drinker opens and closes the lid the origin of "tappit" becomes apparent.

Tazza. See *kylix* in this section.

Third. In the 1400s a third was a form of liquid measure, but like other regional measures it fell from use when the industrial age encouraged standardization.

Thistle cup. A Scottish cup with a single handle, it is like a chalice made of silver with a leafy design around the base.

Thurdendel. Dating back to the end of the seventeenth century, the thurdendel was a drinking vessel of a bit larger than normal capacity to reserve room for the head on the beer. Allowing a little extra room for the head ensured a fair and accurate pour.

Tierce. A cask that held approximately thirty-three gallons, it was also a unit of measure for the same amount.

Toasting glasses. In the early 1700s toasting glasses were made with very narrow and delicate stems. The thin stem allowed those making a toast to easily snap it, destroying the glass and preventing it from being used to make a toast of lesser stature. A later custom of tossing glasses in the fireplace accomplished much the same purpose.

Toby jug. Shaped more like a mug than a jug and designed to resemble a person, Toby mugs have a sizable following of collectors. Throughout the years Toby jugs have borne many different likenesses. Most familiar of all the designs is the image of a slightly rotund and jolly fellow wearing a tricornered hat.

Tokkori. A Japanese bottle with a squat shape that narrows and then flares out again at the mouth. Traditionally used for holding warm sake.

Tonneau. A cask of large design from France, it held the equivalent of 4 hogsheads—about 208 gallons.

Trendle. A word that is out of use now, it was the name of a shallow tub used for cooling beer.

Tun. A large brewery vessel now implying a mash or lautering tank, but in older times a number of wooden barrel-like vessels went by this name. At one time it was also a unit of measure equaling 252 gallons.

Tuplak. A Czechoslovakian glass similar to an English boot. Frequently used in drinking ceremonies.

Tyg. A pottery bowl or glass fitted with multiple handles and used for communal drinking.

Ullage. Void space above a liquid. The volume of the void (headspace) in any vessel. A word to describe empty space in a barrel.

Urna. An ancient Roman liquid measure amounting to half an *amphora,* about 4 1/2 gallons.

Vat. A container generally in the shape of a barrel used by brewers for fermentation, blending, and maturing. As a unit of measure in Belgium and Holland, a vat equals one hectoliter.

Vessel. When spoken of in terms of a brewery, a vessel serves purposes identical to those performed by vats.

Storage vats in an 1847 brewery.

Wager cup. Two different types of drinking vessels went by this name. One was a cup sized as a challenge: It held a considerable volume, which a drinker of respectable capacity could consume in one draft. It was also another name for a puzzle cup.

Whiskin. An English drinking vessel of the 1600s.

Winchester quart. Not a unit of measure, this was actually a bottle holding significantly more than a quart—about five pints—and it was fitted with a glass stopper.

Yard. A famous drinking glass of England. A tall slender glass with a funnel-shaped top and a bulb- or globe-shaped base. It was designed to be handed up to the seated driver of a horse-drawn coach. Use of this glass requires a technique of twisting or swirling the bulb to gently slosh the beer down the flute and funnel-shaped portion, thereby avoiding a sudden gush of beer from the bottom of the glass. Also known as aleyard.

Yull-cawp. Pronounced in the manner of the Ayrshire region popularized by Robert Burns, this was another name for an ale-bowl.

Taverns
and Exalted
Beer Titles

ow did the lowly tavern shape America? The story goes all the way back to the first European settlers. The long voyage to America was a horrifying trial of bad food and drink. Water was not trusted. For years the rivers and streams in Europe were polluted and beer was the only liquid many would drink. For this reason William Bradford noted in his diary that running out of beer on the *Mayflower* caused the Pilgrims to land at Plymouth Rock. It was time to get ashore and start brewing a new supply.

As these newcomers settled, the beer they drank was homebrew. It wasn't until the colonies began exporting goods back to England that beer sales rose to any significant level. Iron, tobacco, and fur brought both beer and hard currency to North America. But even then both were usually restricted to coastal towns and their immediate area.

"Peasants in an Inn," by Van Ostade.

As time passed the Royal Governors grew concerned over the lack of economic activity and development in the crown's interior lands. Merchants might be content limiting trade to the coastal region but it was certainly no way to build and hold an empire. To solve this problem they looked at the development of trade in early England, which was accelerated when it became easier for traders and merchants to travel, meet others, and conduct business in comfortable surroundings. The innovation which caused all this was the venerated English tavern.

Taverns provided a convenient place for travelers to stay and served as a focal point of trade. Because they enabled merchants to expand the range of their business, taverns became centers of commerce. As a result, tavern keepers were among the wealthiest members of any community. So well did this work in England, it seemed only fitting to apply the same solution to the troubled economy of the Americas.

Representatives of the crown soon directed each community to open a tavern or inn to tend the needs of travelers. They knew such action would bring new inhabitants to the undeveloped areas, and right they were. As trade with England and the monetary system further developed, taverns solidified their standing as a community center and no town of any size would be without one.

Colonial administrators must have heartily congratulated themselves over the wisdom of their economic development plan. It was simple to implement, quick to show a return, and required virtually no investment from England. If that weren't enough, the taverns also provided a side benefit not previously considered by the governors, but instrumental to implementing the policy of the crown: a system to administer law.

Burdened by its war debt in Europe, London allocated only a small budget for public works and so government buildings in the colonies were virtually nonexistent. Still, it was essential for any effective colony to be firmly rooted in the practice of English law. The method used to bring government to outlying areas was a system of traveling jurists. As they moved from town to town settling disputes and administering justice it became known as "riding the circuit," and the authority of the crown traveled with them. What better way to administer the law than in the center of a community and in a building that could be used with no expense. Thus it was that taverns became the seat of the local court, making riding the circuit a bit more appealing and further establishing the tavern as a center of any rural community. Overall, it was another triumph for the Royal Governors.

The role of the tavern as both a legal and commercial center had an unparalleled impact on colonial development. Since the growth and conduct of a region's affairs were tied to the tavern, it was not long until it was also the social focus of a region. Travelers invariably brought news, and through this system the colonials maintained contact with the mother country. But this was not the limit of the tavern's role. Among the other benefits it provided was a means of common defense.

In colonial times it was the ordinary citizenry which banded together into a militia. But such an army brought problems of inconsistency in both ability and experience of its members. However, with problems of its own back on the continent, powers in London were reluctant to station a standing army in America.

Thus defense was left to the colonists, except that when faced with a choice, most militia members avoided the supposedly mandatory training days. The attitude seemed to be an unspoken "Well of course I'll take this serious . . . when I'm faced with certain death." Unfortunately, an army is ineffective and subject to slaughter if it cannot maneuver with speed and discipline in the field. However, neither pleas nor demands corrected the problem. The frontier inhabitants simply wouldn't show up for training.

Finally, the governors turned to a solution that had successfully solved other colonial problems—beer. Need to turn out the population of a region? Easy, underwrite a few barrels of beer at the local tavern. It was an immediate success and able-bodied militiamen literally appeared out of the colonial woodwork. It wasn't long until Drill Day became a not-to-be-missed social function of the North American frontier. And eventually they learned not to dispense free beer until the training was complete.

Through their ordeals with army life the citizen soldiers were learning a few things. First, they could function on their own. Second, they were learning to both assemble and operate as a unit out of a central point, the tavern.

Indeed, it was from a tavern that a mob spilled out to provoke the Boston's British garrison into what became known as The Boston Massacre. Later, from a planning and command post in Boston's Green Dragon Tavern, they launched a protest to taxes which became known as the Boston Tea Party. Such disregard for property, at the hands of an organized mob, pushed the crown to the limits of its tolerance and set the stage for military action.

When the two sides met in Lexington, Massachusetts, the opening of hostilities took place in exactly the fashion in which the militia was trained. Their leader, Captain Parker, established his headquarters in the nearby Buckman Tavern.

Thus part of the solution to colonial development, encouraging the growth of taverns, eventually led to the end of British colonial America. And it all happened because of beer.

Ale bench. Placed outside the local tavern, inn, or alehouse, this was a low bench upon which the owner, brewer, and regulars of the village were frequently spotted drinking and relaxing.

Ale conner. An old title for one who inspected, and tasted, ale. The position was created to ensure ale met the standard for quality set forth by law.

The ale conner's oath.

You shall swear, that you know of no brewer, or brewster, cook, or pie-baker, in your ward, who sells the gallon of best ale for more than one penny halfpenny, or the gallon of second for more than one penny, or otherwise than by measure sealed and full of clear ale; or who brews less than he used to do before this cry, by reason hereof, or withdraws himself from fol-

The ale conner tested the quality of beer by pouring some on a bench and sitting on it. If it stuck to his leather trousers it indicated the quality of the ale.

lowing his trade the rather by reason of this cry; or if any persons shall do contrary to any one of these points, you shall certify the Alderman of your ward and of their names. And that you, so soon as you shall be required to taste any ale of a brewer or brewster, shall be ready to do the same; and in case that it be less good than it used to be before this cry, you, by assent of your Alderman, shall set a reasonable price thereon, according to your discretion; and if any one shall afterwards sell the same above the said price, unto your Alderman you shall certify the same. And that for gift, promise, knowledge, hare or other cause whatsoever, no brewer, brewster, huckster, cook, or pie-baker, who acts against any one of the points aforesaid, you shall conceal, spare or tortuously aggrieve; nor when you are required to taste ale, shall absent yourself without reasonable cause and true; but all things which unto your office pertains to do, you shall well and lawfully do. So God you help, and all the saints.

(Liber Albus [1419])

The appointment of ale conners in England dates back to the times and charter of William the Conqueror. Shakespeare's father was reputed to hold the office of ale conner. The question remains to this day: Where do you apply for such a job?

Ale drapper. An outdated name for the keeper of an alehouse.

Ale garland. One of the ways in medieval England, where the general population could not read, to advertise the operation of an alehouse. It was a bush or garland placed atop a pole in front of the alehouse.

Alehouse. An old English name for a tavern that sold ale. It was a barlike establishment not as extensively appointed as an inn.

Ale knight. A title given to one who was emboldened through the power of ale. In other words, a title given to a man fortified with Dutch courage.

Come all you brave wights
That are dubbed ale Knights

Most frequently this form of knighthood was bestowed following bouts of overconsumption. One writer of the 1600s wrote: "I know some aleknights so much addicted thereunto, that they will not cease from morow until even . . . to stirre from their stooles, wit still pinking with their narrow eies as halfe sleeping, till the fume of their adversarie be digested that he may go to it afresh."

Ale passion. Caused by too much passion for ale. An old term for a hangover. No doubt ale knights were titled one night and automatically received this dubious honor the next morning. This condition was also called "kicked by the brewer's horse."

Ale pole. The pole placed in front on an alehouse. A means to let a non-literate public know where they could buy beer. An older equivalent of the neon shape of a beer mug.

Ale stake. In the days of widespread illiteracy, this long pole, with a bushy branch attached, was placed in front of a brewery to indicate to the ale conner that the latest brew was ready for inspection. Later it was used as a sort of crude sign to indicate a tavern. See *ale garland* in this section.

Ale wife. From ancient to medieval times brewing was always entrusted to women. In England this was a woman brewer's title. See *brewster* in this section.

Alewright. In medieval England people who worked in a trade often went by the title "wright," and in the 1600s alewright was one of the titles applied to brewers.

Anchor Brewery. Why mention a brewery in this section? Because of its larger historical context. Mention of the name Anchor to modern cerevisaphiles brings the San Francisco brewery to mind, but this Anchor Brewery predates that one by centuries and deserves mention here because it was associated with a tavern.

In medieval England, a society recovering from the black plague was learning to build an economy, and one device that worked better than anything else to promote trade was the local inn or tavern. It provided traveling merchants not only the nourishment and comfort of beer but also sleeping quarters, meals, and stables. Later, when competition among taverns increased, entertainment was added. One tavern of old London grew so popular that it was known more for its entertainment than its beer, although the beer was always there. During one performance a cannon used as a prop during a performance of *Henry V* set fire to the stage. Those standing in the area that then contained the cheap seats tried to extinguish it with beer, but, alas, it burned down. No doubt not enough were willing to sacrifice their beer to save a theater. After the fire the theater never reopened, but the brewery did. It was known first as the Anchor and later as Thrales (and listed the famous Samuel Johnson as an investor). Within the brewery stood a storehouse for porter off an internal alley named after the old theater. Of course, the brewery has disappeared. It had to go, because local authorities figured it was important to build a re-creation of the old theater. You've probably heard of it. It was called the Globe, and a playwright named Will Shakespeare had a fair number of plays running there. Let's hope they make it genuinely authentic and bring back the beer concession.

Bar. The name applied to a public counter dedicated to the sale of alcoholic beverages. Its origins remain clouded in mystery. Although some claim it was originally used in the legal profession as a reference to the rail that separated court-recognized lawyers from lawyers who were not recognized, an equal case could be made for its use in a pub to keep the customers a controllable working distance from the products.

Bar engine. A piston pump integral to the bar's tap and designed specifically for use in drawing a beer up from the cellar cask to the tap at the bar. The term "pulling a draft" comes from the name of this device. Also known as a beer pull, it works much like an old-fashioned water pump.

Barkeep. See *barman* and *barmaid* in this section.

Barley Island. An obsolete term. It doesn't take much imagination to see how it was used centuries ago as the veiled name for an alehouse. Oh what a fate to be stranded on Barley Island!

Barmaid. The feminine equivalent of barman.

Barman. The name for an attendant (not necessarily the owner) of a tavern serving patrons and minding the bar.

Barmy. A term used to describe a person who is not quite right in the head. *Barm* was an old word for the head on a beer. Thus, to be "barmy" is to have a head full of bubbles.

Bar parlour. No longer in popular use, the term referred to a small, well-appointed part of a bar, tavern, or inn that was reserved for the most regular, and thus privileged, customers.

Bar-spoon. Generally, a long-handled spoon used to mix and stir various drinks. The spoon used in preparation of a black and tan can also be called a bar-spoon.

Bartender. A more modern, and American, term for a barman.

Beer garden. Now thought of as a place to enjoy a beer outdoors. In the days before refrigeration, a way to keep the ground above a brewery's aging cellar cool was to plant a grove of shade trees there. Breweries would often sell their beer outdoors in the "garden," and hence the modern application of the name.

Beer house. A term most closely associated with the United Kingdom, it refers to an establishment that sells beer but no spirits or other liquors.

Beer money. Rations of beer supplied to the British armed forces. In the case beer was not available for the daily ration, an allowance would be paid in lieu. This amounted to about a penny per day. The custom ran from 1800 to its abolishment in 1873.

Beer pull. Another name for a beer engine, a hand-powered pump that pulls beer up from the cask in the cellar to the tap at the bar.

Bending the elbow. This was and remains a term used to describe a seriously dedicated beer drinker. Some people are called elbow benders, and the act has sometimes been called "doing twelve-ounce curls."

Throughout Europe beer lovers have, through the centuries, enthusiastically raised a glass in beer gardens.

Biber. A person who frequently drinks to excess, but not necessarily a drunkard. This term has become slightly antiquated.

The bierkieser.

Bierkieser. An appointed post in German Alsace equivalent to an ale conner. The position was established between 1723 and 1763. During that period the region instituted a law similar to the *Reinheitsgebot* (German beer purity law of 1516), which allowed only malt, hops, and water as ingredients. The use of anything else to produce beer was a punishable offense. The job of the bierkieser was to taste newly tapped beer and ensure it met standards of quality. We want to know how one applies for such a job.

Bierstube. A German word meaning "beer room." However, the term has a much broader meaning as a chamber designated for drink, food, fun, and music.

"The Fountain"—a San Francisco version of a bierstube from 1879.

Bit sikari. Ancient Sumerian beer shops and taverns were named *bit sikari*, which identified them as places to get beer.

Boniface. An out-of-date title for an innkeeper. The use originated with the landlord character in George Farquhar's play, *The Beaux' Stratagem* (1707).

Breweriana. Any of the beer- or brewery-related artifacts and mementos sought after by enthusiasts and collectors. It may include coasters, trays, labels, cans, tankards, steins, tap handles, and the like. Often, bars and brewpubs feature displays of breweriana.

Brewster. The old English word for a woman brewer. The job of brewing beer belonged to women for most of early history. Alreck, king of Hordoland, was said to have chosen his queen by her ability to brew.

Brother bung. Alehouse slang from England that refers either to a drinking buddy or a brewer.

Bush. Another word for the old symbols used to advertise inns. See *ale stake* and *ale pole* in this section.

Bush-house. A temporary brewery or alehouse set on the site of a fair and designated by placing a bush out front, much in the style of an ale stake.

Cellar. In the days before refrigeration, the best place to keep beer cool was below ground. Brewers took advantage of the cool earth by constructing breweries set back into the sides of hills. The insulating properties of the dirt-surrounded cellar kept the temperature stable for a long period of time. Taverns, too, used cellars for storing beer, and the term "cellar temperature" refers to the 50 °F or so found in most cellars.

Cellarman. The employee of a tavern charged with the storage and care of beer in the cellar. The position holds great responsibility in bars that specialize in cask-conditioned ales. Cask, or "real," beers possess a delicate nature and require great care. The cellarman must, through skill and experience, determine how much pressure the cask should retain, how long it should be allowed to settle, and when to tap the keg for sale.

Cellar temperature. Often mistaken as "warm," in actuality cellar temperature represents a temperature of about 50 °F. This temperature adequately protects an ale from damage and allows serving in a condition that presents its character best.

Cerevisaphile. A beer enthusiast, lover, or fan.

Chafer-house. In England this term was a name for an alehouse. It probably referred to the saucepans used in the kitchen.

Cheese. In old writings the word *cheese* in the context of a tavern does not necessarily imply a dairy product. Most commonly it was a large wooden ball found in the popular tavern game of skittles.

Chevaliers de Malte. A title originated by a Frenchman of the 1700s as a designation for brewers. *Chevalier* in French translates as "knight"— very fitting indeed.

Chin-chin. Neither a piece of tavern equipment nor any appointment found in a tavern, nevertheless it was a common part of the old tavern experience. Chin-chin was a salutation or toast as common in the taverns existent between the 1800s and early 1900s, and perhaps more so, than the modern equivalent in England of "cheers."

Ciborium. An obsolete name for a glass used for a variety of drinks. It was originally shaped somewhat like a chalice.

Club. Different from the modern sense, of *nightclub,* this was the term once used in England to describe a drinking party or group in which members would share the cost of drinking. Think of it as a more organized version of the college practice of throwing money in the hat to buy a keg.

Cock-a-hoop. In medieval England the great majority of the populace could not read, and the common means of identifying things, including alehouses, was through symbols. In its earliest form, the alehouse was identified by a stake with a bush tied to the top. The ale stake evolved into simple signs, the first of which was the cock-a-hoop. Placing the bird inside a hoop was a reference to a beer barrel. Barrels, casks, and kegs of the era were made of wood staves held together by encircling bands, or hoops, of bent wood or metal. When the keg was laid on its side in the alehouse the barkeep would pour beer from the keg by inserting a tap, which included a valve known as a "cock." Thus, an ale drapper would advertise his goods on a sign that depicted the cock and the hoop.

Cock and bull stories. Associated with rumor, this label for an outrageous or unbelievable tale originated in taverns or, more specifically, between two taverns. In centuries past, on the main road to London two taverns stood directly across the road from each other. As stages stopped to rest the horses, passengers drew pints of ale and mingled about in the road, drinking ale and relating news items to one another. Of course, those bits of news had passed through a series of mouths and were embellished in each telling. Soon the stories assumed an altered state that bore little resemblance to the truth. Thus, news coming into town via that route was, over time, looked at with deserved skepticism.

Ale sellers should not be tale tellers.

(Old proverb)

Before long, any wild story was characterized with the names of those two neighboring taverns—the Cock and the Bull. Today the beer-related meaning has faded, but the term *cock and bull* story has a secure spot in our language.

Comb. As you would run a comb across your head, so too barkeeps of old used a comb on beer. Often provided free to bars as a promotional item from a brewery, combs were tools of the trade. A simple device, a beer comb resembled a tongue depressor with a slight curve. Combs scraped the excess head off a freshly poured beer.

Commissatio. An ancient Roman drinking party that implies excess in the conduct of the participants.

Coopers. The title for one engaged in the profession of barrel making. Before the age of metal kegs, a brewery employed scores of coopers to construct and repair their casks. Shaping and fitting the gracefully curved staves of a barrel required great skill, and coopers were an invaluable part of the brewery's staff.

Crawler. More popularly used in the United Kingdom than the United States, the term describes anyone engaged in the activity of pub crawling.

Crossing the Yuba. An outdated expression used as a popular toast in California during the mid-1800s. It was a phrase of the times, when immigrants flocked to the West Coast in droves.

Dadloms. A miniature-sized game of skittles frequently seen in bar rooms and taverns. It uses a scaled-down cheese. See *cheese* and *skittles* in this section.

Darts. A game thought to have originated as a test of knife-throwing skill, where darts first appeared is not known. The game first rose to prominence at the court of Henry II of England. It did not gain widespread acceptance with the masses until the latter half of the 1800s. Now popular in taverns around the world, a couple of dozen variations have been invented for play on a standard board.

Dart widow. A reference to the spouse waiting at home while the other half occupies a spot at the pub engrossed in darts and a few pints.

Dead house. A type of hotel associated with one of the less desirable aspects of taverns. It was a place where "dead-drunks" could sleep off the effects of overindulgence.

Devil among the tailors. Used by many as an alternate name for the tavern game of skittles, in the case of the devil among the tailors the cheese was called the devil. See *skittles* in this section.

Devil's chapel. Playing upon the historically close connection between religion and beer, wags of the Middle Ages used this term with a wink and a nod in referring to the local tavern. At that time alehouses were often physically attached to the local church.

Dive. A modern slang term for a low-class or run-down bar. In the 1700s in England it indicated an inexpensive bar. The name originated from the location of the bar, usually in the basement of a building. Affordable meals consisting of sausages, tripe, and boiled beef were standard fare and were washed down with jacks of beer.

Dividend. Similar to a club or drinking party, all associated with a dividend paid in a set fee to purchase ale during the 1700s, which was then made available to all members. See *club* and *everlasting club* in this section.

Draught. The British spelling of "draft." Purists restrict the use to "real ale"—a cask-conditioned beer.

Drayman. Invaluable to breweries from the Middle to the Industrial Ages, a drayman was the brewery's deliveryman. At one time a brewer had to have stables full of horses and men to care for them and make rounds of the accounts. With the introduction of mechanized transportation, the draymen, their horses, and their carts slowly disappeared from brewing. Horse-drawn beer wagons and associated draymen remaining at modern breweries serve a largely traditional and ceremonial role.

Dutch. The customary manner of drinking, in which each individual pays his or her own way.

Egart. A position in the 1500s and 1600s that is similar to an ale conner. The person responsible for evaluating the quality of beer that is sold.

A group of egarts, or ale conners, relaxing over a beer.

Elbow bending. A euphemism so commonly used and universally understood that it has become synonymous with drinking.

Eswart. As with egart, another of the titles given to an ale conner, one responsible for judging the quality of beer to be sold.

Everlasting club. Odd as it may seem, this kind of drinking club had an objective of keeping at least one member always drinking an ale. Night and day the members were organized and scheduled to relieve each other in their duties at the tavern. One observation from the early 1700s described their ability and activities:

> Since their first institution they have smoked fifty tons of tobacco, drank thirty thousand butts of ale, one thousand hogsheads of red port, two hundred barrels of brandy, and one kilderkine of small beer. They sang old catches at all hours to encourage one another to moisten their clay, and grow immortal by drinking.

A kilderkin equals eighteen gallons, thus its mention was both a joke and a swipe at small beer. See *kilderkin* in the Beer Bottles, Barrels, Glasses, Vessels, and Measures section.

Expenses. A loosely used reference to all forms of bar or drinking money, which includes tipping and entertainments, that dates from the Elizabethan period.

Extension. When used in the context of operating a tavern, this was special permission to remain open later than the normal licensing hours. Extensions were granted for national holidays, special celebrations and feasts, and other occasions of importance.

Flap dragoning. The practice of floating a flammable substance on top of beer, lighting it, and drinking it in one draft. In modern times the beer is often omitted and other names apply to the custom; however, it was originally a sort of tavern sport.

Four-ale bar. At first this was the name for English taverns that served mild ale, but in later centuries it was used interchangeably with tavern, inn, or alehouse. It has fallen from common use.

Free house. Not applied to bars in the United States, where a three-tier system exists and law prevents breweries and distilleries from owning bars. It remains in use throughout the United Kingdom as an informal designation for any pub not owned by a beverage company and therefore operating with the freedom to sell any brand.

Froth-blower. A member of the Ancient Order of Froth Blowers. Something of a ceremonial group, this is a type of fraternal drinking organization.

Gambrinus. The patron of beer lovers. The name is a corruption of medieval Jan Primus, who was a nobleman of medieval Belgium, which was then part of the Netherlands. He was one of the first to endorse a guild of brewers. One theory on the corruption of the name to Gambrinus holds that this name came from the medieval German *gambra*, a word meaning "germination of grain," the process that turns barley into brewing malt. This explanation seems plausible when taken in the context of the poem "The Origin of Beer":

Gambrinus is known as both the king and patron of beer.

In a jolly field of barley
King Gambrinus slept,
And dreaming of his thirsty realm
the merry monarch wept,
'in all my land of Netherland
there grows no mead or wine,
And water I could never coax
adown this throat of mine . . .

(an angel then tells him)

"In the barley where thou sleepest
there hides a nectar clear,
Which men shall know in later times
as porter, ale or beer"

(an anonymous Saxon)

Gambrinus holds a place of respect among brewers and the beer-drinking public of the world.

Ganymede. In classical Greek mythology, Ganymede was a youth who served as cupbearer to the gods. See *Hebe* in this section.

Globe Theater. Shakespeare in the tavern section? Well, at one time they did serve beer during the performances. For a complete explanation of the Globe's tie to beer, see *Anchor Brewery* in this section.

Goudalier. From medieval France, this was the title for merchants who sold "good" beer—good ale'ers.

Growler. Once, the growler was the most popular form of beer take-out. Shaped like a bucket with a press-on or hinged metal lid, before the advent of the six-pack it was the manner in which beer drinkers carried beer home. It was also the basis for a phrase once popular in America, "rushing the growler." During the late 1800s and first half of the 1900s, children were sent on the errand of running to the tavern with an empty growler and returning home with a full one. They were instructed to "Rush the growler." See *growler* in the Beer Bottles, Barrles, Glasses, Vessels, and Measures section.

Hebe. In classical mythology, a Greek goddess who was a cupbearer to the gods and was also the goddess of youth. The word came to be applied to a barmaid or woman tavern keeper.

Highgate oath. One of the many drinking customs commonly found in the fraternal atmosphere of an English tavern. It originated from a group or club of cattlemen with exclusive membership that would only admit new members if they had passed an initiation, the highlight of which was to kiss an oxen between the horns. As time passed, the ritual evolved into a merriment administered to travelers passing through Highgate on the way to London. In the more merry version the travelers were led before a pair of horns (drinking vessels) and made to swear an oath that they would never drink small beer when strong was available.

> *. . . many to the steep of Highgae hie;*
> *Ask ye, Boetotian shades, the reason why?*
> *'Tis to the worship of the solemn horn,*
> *Graped in the holy hand of Mystery,*
> *In whose dread name both men and maids are sworn,*
> *And consecrate the oath wih draught and dance till morn.*

The Highgate oath is not an isolated phenomenon—similar types of drinking societies were once a widespread part of English tavern life.

Hobnob. Socializing and "hobnobbing" were both born in the tavern. As the center of a community, the tavern was the place where friends met. In Old English, "habbe or nabbe" asked the critical question "Will you have or not have a drink?" As the language evolved, hobnob became the acceptable pronunciation. Since that time its use has changed slightly to a broader sense of socializing.

Hoop. In the days when an overwhelming majority of the British population was illiterate, a hoop hanging in front of an alehouse told people that barrels of ale were available inside. It was an intermediate step between the use of an ale stake and the signboards that would appear later. See *ale stake, ale pole*, and *cock-a-hoop* in this section.

Hop pillow. An actual pillow, but instead of feathers, it was stuffed with hops. It was an English home cure from the 1600s to the early 1700s that recommended hop pillows as a way to both encourage and enhance sleep.

Hukster. A woman of medieval England who would buy ale from the local brewster and then resell it to the beer-drinking public.

King John's Palace of Colnbrook is an example of a classic English inn.

Inn. A version of the tavern with rooms and stables attached. The inn gets credit for spreading trade, civilization, and the popularity of beers. Inns were more than a bar—they offered travelers a place to get refreshment, rooms, meals, and, of course, beer.

> *He goes not out of his way that goes to a good inn.*
>
> (George Herbert [1640])

Eventually the inn became, like the tavern, a place for social gatherings and often included entertainment.

> *There is nothing which has been contrived by man*
> *by which so much happiness is produced as by a good tavern or inn.*
>
> (Samuel Johnson)

Inns were also known as the place for local sporting clubs and other organizations to assemble.

Inn keeper. The owner or manager of an inn who performed duties similar to those of a tavern keeper, but with responsibilities that also included the running of a hotel.

Inn signs. When most of the general population in England could read, signs were used to announce the location of a bar or inn, rather than a physical object such as a garland or bush.

Kicked by the brewer's horse. A great headache, specifically one brought on by overindulgence. Also known as ale passion.

Ku-Baba. Famed brewster (female brewer) and tavern keeper of Sumer in 2400 B.C. She was noted for founding the ancient city of Kish, northeast of Babylon. Her name appears in conjunction with beer repeatedly in ancient texts.

Landlord. Unofficial but widespread English title usually given to a tavern's licensee despite the fact that a brewery may actually own the building. Another name for a tavern keeper.

Lickspigot. An English name, now out of use, for a tavern or alehouse keeper.

Local. A slang term affectionately applied in England to the neighborhood "local" pub or tavern.

Loggerhead. Every good English and colonial tavern had a loggerhead stationed by the fireplace. Made of iron and resembling a fireplace poker, loggerheads had a special relationship with beer. In the days when beer mixed drinks were at the height of their popularity, a loggerhead was thrust into the embers as the tavern keeper blended ingredients in his own special rendition of the drink ordered. When it was thoroughly mixed, he would retrieve the glowing loggerhead and thrust it into the tankard for a final stir. The heated loggerhead accomplished two things: It heated the drink and it caramelized some of the sugars. Flip was the most famous drink using a heated loggerhead. In more modern language, to be at loggerheads refers to the spirited arguments that often resulted from drinking bouts.

Long pull. An extrafull serving of beer. For the origin of the word, see *long pull* in the Beer Bottles, Barrels, Glasses, Vessels, and Measures section.

Lounge. Typically, this was the best-appointed and most luxurious section of a pub or bar. It was usually reserved for the most affluent customers.

Maltman. An alternative and infrequently used term in the United States for a maltster.

Maltster. A person engaged in the profession of malting barley.

Monks. Throughout the Middle Ages it was the Catholic Church that maintained knowledge of brewing and introduced advances in making beer. Monks were beer's greatest guardians and some of its biggest enthusiasts. The character of Friar Tuck in *Ivanhoe* was a likely representation of the monks of the period when the king says to him: ". . . and three hogsheads of ale of the first strike [strong ale]. And if that will not quench thy thirst, thou must come to court, and be acquainted with my butler."

Muggling. Curious old drinking game played in the English countryside during the 1600s. A group of six beer lovers would get together and begin drinking rounds. The first person would drink one glass of beer, the second person two, the third three, and so on. When the glass came back to the first person the number to be consumed was seven glasses, followed by the next person with eight, and continuing around again and again until only one person was left standing. Obviously, muggling proves that not all foolish beer-drinking customs were invented in college.

Mughouse. A drinking establishment much like a tavern or music hall, in which only ale was served. Though once a hotbed of political activity, the mughouse changed over the years and eventually lost completely that original association. A description from 1722 of one of the mughouses depicts nothing close to an organized political meeting.

> *Here is nothing drunk but ale, and every gentleman hath his separate Mug,*
> *which he chalks on the table where he sits as it is brought in . . .*
> *drinking from one table to another to one another's health's*
> *that there is no room for Politicks. . . .*
> *One must be there by even to get Room. . . .*
> *This is a winter's amusement, that is agreeable enough to a stranger.*

Only a few years later the political purpose of the mughouse was revived as a means for tradesmen to fight against the Tories. Eventually their activism led to a series of riots that were finally put down by police using no less a deterrent than physical destruction of the mughouses. As time passed the mughouses went through several cycles of functioning as a place for social gatherings and than as a meeting place of groups with various quasi-political affiliations. Also known as a mugroom.

Mugroom. A synonym for mughouse.

Muller. An essential piece of tavern gear in the sixteenth and seventeenth centuries, this was a large, sturdy vessel used in the preparation of mulled drinks. See *mulled* in the Beer-Based Mixed Drinks section.

Mullet. Shaped like a funnel with the narrow part closed, this tool was found near a tavern's fireplace, where it was filled with beer and placed in the fire for heating. When warm, the beer was used to make mixed drinks.

Multitap bars. Establishments with a large number of draft beer lines often call themselves multitap bars. Commonly, the term identifies those bars with a large selection of craft-brewed beers.

Newsroom. Colonial American taverns and English pubs of the same era often had one room that bore the unofficial name of "newsroom." It was so called because the newspapers it contained were a luxury for most people of those times. However, most taverns, as the center of a community's social life, would serve also to distribute the news.

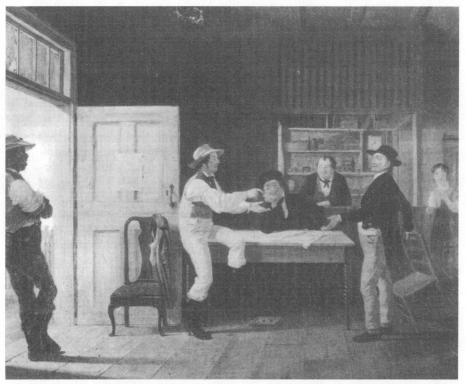

Colonial taprooms served as the newrooms of the day and as centers for political discussion.

Nine men's monies. A fashionable tavern game of the Elizabethan era that used counters or marbles on a game board to keep score. Some contend it was a type of board game in which markers were rolled on a grid to score points.

Nine pins. A barroom bowling game that once enjoyed great popularity. Related to skittles, nine pins was a game once found in taverns throughout England.

October Club. Members were noted for their love of October ale. Not your run-of-the-mill beer swillers, these were Tory members of Parliament, numbering more than one hundred, who met over mugs of their favorite ale to plot disruptions of the opposing (Whig) party.

Ordinary. English taverns once had a custom of serving meals at a fixed price. The meal was called an ordinary, and it included unlimited servings of ale. As time passed the common and less expensive beer served with the meal assumed the name. Patrons would order it by asking for an "ordinary." See *ordinary bitter* in the Beers and Beer Drinking section.

Paebi. In ancient civilizations the brewers held places of honor. *Paebi* is a word from ancient Mesopotamia that loosely translates to "the royal brewer."

Parlour. An old English designation for the best room in a pub or tavern. A barkeep would reserve the parlour for use by only his very best customers. It was also known as the lounge.

Pig and Whistle. Very popular as a name for English taverns. It was thought to have derived from a type of tankard called a piggin. The phrase in which it gained fame was "piggin wassail," or "a tankard of wassail," quite a proper and acceptable manner in which to toast the season.

Porterhouse. When porter was first introduced, the taverns that served it became known as Porter Houses. However, as time went by, the name was assumed by the choice cut of beef the porterhouses were known for serving. Today the name of the original taverns lives on in the porterhouse steak.

Pot boy. Title for a young man working in an English alehouse or tavern. The pot boys filled the role of what would later be called a waiter or waitress, running pots (earthen tankards) of ale out to the patrons and bringing back the empties.

A pot boy (left) delivers beers to patrons.

Pot-house. Inferior to a tavern, inn, or pub, the pot-house was a low-grade alehouse. Completely lacking in appointments, atmosphere, and other diversions, it was a place for drinking and only drinking. Think of it as a dive.

Pot knight. Similar in meaning to an ale knight. A pot was the name of a drinking vessel, and drinkers emboldened after overconsumption were called pot knights.

Potman. Title bestowed upon a tavern or barkeeper's assistant. It was derived from the old name for a drinking vessel called a pot.

Pot valor. Derived from the same meaning as was pot knight. This was a reference to liquid courage found during a bout of overconsumption.

Ps and Qs. Tavern keepers in the days before cash registers and running tabs would have each waiter and waitress keep a count of how much beer was served to a group by marking the Ps (pints) and Qs (quarts) on a tally slate. Occasionally, especially during raucous and crowded times, the tavern keeper would remind the staff to pay close attention to business by the phrase "mind your Ps and Qs," verbal shorthand for "Remember to keep an accurate tally of your served Pints and Quarts." That method of telling people to mind the conduct of business evolved into a slang term with a meaning of "be on your best behavior."

Red lattice. Now outdated, red lattice was once a synonym for an English alehouse between the late 1500s and late 1600s. In old times nearly all alehouses had windows that opened directly onto the street. To offer the patrons privacy while maintaining ventilation, tavern owners installed a lattice in front of the window. Acting like a screen, it prevented those on the street from seeing in, although those inside had a fine view looking out. One writer observed, "He called me . . . through a red lattice, and I could see no part of his face from the window; at last I spied his eyes and me thought he had made two holes in the ale-wife's new petticoat, and peeped through."

Rough. Tavern keepers used this word for the spillage that occurred when drawing a draft beer. It was, of course, something they wanted to avoid.

Round. An order of drinks for everyone in a group. The term comes apparently from the old custom of passing around a communal drinking bowl or tankard.

Saloon. In America this word signifies an establishment licensed for on-premise consumption with little emphasis on food, if any. In the British Isles the saloon provides a better bar than does an ordinary pub.

Scantling. A type of wooden cradle used to hold casks once went by this name.

Schenke. The German word for tavern.

School. Euphemistically, a group of people engaged in buying rounds of beer.

Sconce. Originating in English universities, sconcing was a traditional means of paying a forfeit for any violation of etiquette. A person "sconced" in either beer or money.

Scot ale. A phrase used to describe an action rather than a beer. In medieval times English forest officers, who maintained their own taverns, required travelers passing through their jurisdiction to drink in their ale-houses. It was a way of earning a little extra money on the side. "You say you want safe passage through this dark and scary forest? No problem. Relax and have a beer, then I'll see to it you get through just fine."

Shout. Barroom slang for buying a round of drinks. The term is thought to be a reflection of the loud call (to the barkeep and the drinkers) from the buyer.

Shove groat. A game played in the alehouses of old England, it used coins called *groat* that were rolled down a board to score points.

Shove ha'penny. A tavern game that was a direct descendent of shove groat.

Sizing. Food and drink ordered from a college's pantry.

Skittles. Old English tavern entertainment, a type of game similar to bowling nine pins with a ball called a cheese. It was also known as devil among the tailors.

Snug. A small semiprivate room situated separately from but adjacent to a pub's barroom. In older custom it was used as a sitting room reserved for the ladies. Also called a snuggery.

Stoss an. A German beer drinker's exclamation, which translates to "clink glasses."

Symposium. From the ancient Greek, a euphemism for a drinking bout.

Tap. As a noun, it is the same as a spigot, the wooden valve (stopcock) inserted in a plugged hole in the butt of a barrel and then used to draw off the beer. As a verb it is the act of installing or inserting the tap or spigot into the keg. The term "tapping a keg" survives despite the replacement of wooden kegs with aluminum and, now, steel.

Tapas. Light snacks provided gratis by a European pub or bar. A pleasant tradition. Unfortunately it is more common in European bars than in American ones.

Taproom. Essentially, the same as the barroom. Historically, the room in a tavern or inn where the draft beer was poured and served.

Tapster. An outmoded title once applied to the barman of a pub or tavern.

Tavern. From the Latin *taberna* (hut or inn), the place for public gatherings as the world left the Dark Ages and formed the critical corner to the triangle of the three Ts—trade, travel, and taverns.

A tavern is a common consumption of the afternoon and the murderer . . .
of a rainy day. It is the busy man's recreation,
the idle man's business, the melancholy man's sanctuary,
the stranger's welcome, the inns of court man's entertainment,
the scholar's kindness, and the citizen's country.

(Reuben and Sholto Percy)

In the Dark Ages in Europe, taverns were built alongside the old Roman roads. More than anything else, taverns opened up the world, the minds of its inhabitants, the concept of entertainment, and more than a few bottles of beer. Other colloquial words for tavern include taberna, buttery, wine cellar, tap house, kitchen, hostry, and parlour.

Tavern keeper. A publican or barkeep. It was the title of one who owned or ran the tavern. A publican might not serve meals, but a tavern keeper usually operated a restaurant along with the bar.

Tavern tale. A story or questionable report heard in a tavern, generally over a couple of pints. Tavern tales were not considered reliable information. See *cock and bull stories* in this section.

Tied house. The name for a tavern or pub either owned by a brewery or carrying only one brewery's product through a formal business arrangement. Tied houses were outlawed in the United States following Prohibition, but the practice remains active in Europe.

Toast. This custom most likely had its origin with wassail and communal drinking around the holidays, when it was natural to wish others the best of luck in the upcoming year. Wassail was accompanied by bits of spiced cake or toast added in its preparation. From this came *toast,* meaning to propose a drink in honor of someone or something.

Vast toasts on the delicious lake,
Like ships at sea, may swim.

(*Earl of Rochester*)

Topes. A synonym for toast.

Tsabitu. A female tavern keeper of ancient Sumer.

Typella. Much like ale drapper, this was the name once applied to a barman or seller of ale. The title was derived from *typhyle*, what was, in the Middle Ages, the English word for ale.

Vomitorium. Yes there was such a thing. Adjacent to some Roman dining rooms, it provided relief to revelers who may have overindulged in food, or drink, or both.

The Good Word—
Quotes and Toasts
Worth Repeating

rom the start, civilizations were captivated by the magic of brewing. Truly thankful for a gift they believed came from the gods, they incorporated beer into the most solemn aspects of their religion. From Sumer the epic poem "Ode to Ninkasi" functioned as a testament to their goddess of brewing. It both praised the gift of beer and provided a detailed account of brewing procedures. During a time when writing was no easy chore, putting brewing practices to papyrus, or literally carving it in stone, spoke volumes about beer's importance in daily life.

As the centuries progressed beer's status remained secure in the words and events of history. It appeared in the writings of the Egyptians, Greeks, and Romans. Later, the Irish embraced beer, and it was they who spread brewing knowledge across Europe in the smoldering ashes of the Roman Empire.

On through the Middle Ages and the Renaissance, beer supplied nourishment and inspiration to the intellectually thirsty. It appeared in novels, plays, poems, and songs as the common thread of society's fabric.

Over time beer's official role in religion diminished, but unofficially it flourished in a ritual performed to ward off evil spirits and ensure good health—the toast. The toast received its name from a drinking practice in which a bit of toasted bread was dropped in a glass of beer. As much as written word enhanced the position of beer, the toast solidified its place in culture. A good toast could inspire and encourage, declare friendship and love, and offer vows of dedication. Toasts eased the sorrow of parting and greeted heartfelt reunions. They welcomed new members of a family and punctuated the grieving of those lost to death.

Beer has been a faithful companion to all that makes living worthwhile, and along the way it has provided the means for truly inspired speech. Numerous memorable phrases, praises, and toasts come from throughout the ages and from time's best-known voices, and it was beer that touched them all.

Henry Aldrich (1648–1710)

If all be true that I do think,
There are five reasons we should drink;
Good wine—a friend—or being dry—
Or lest we should be by and by—
Or any other reason why.

H. Warner Allen

Give a young man a twenty-mile tramp and a few pints of good beer, and he has nothing to envy for sheer animal content in the connoisseur's intellectual ecstasies over a great wine.

Woody Allen

I'm the guy who comes home from work, takes his shirt off, opens a bottle of beer, and turns on the Knicks game.

Amphis (from a manuscript fragment, 330 B.C.)

Drink and be merry, for our time on earth is short, and death lasts for ever.

Anacreon

Anacreon was an ancient Greek poet famous for drink-related verse. Anacreon societies (drinking clubs) were once popular. Members of these societies would compose lyrics in praise of drink. One of these verses, written by John Stafford Smith of London, would become the basis of the *Star Spangled Banner*.

Anonymous

Cervesariis feliciter is an ancient Roman saying that translates to "long life to the brewers."

Anonymous

"Bung ho!" An old English bar toast.

Anonymous

Bread is the staff of life, but beer is life itself.

Anonymous

When treading London's well-known ground
If e'er I feel my spirits tire,
I haul my sail, look up around,
In search of Whitbreads' best entire.

Anonymous

No man is drunk so long as he can lie on the floor without holding on.

Anonymous

They speak of my drinking, but never of my thirst.

Anonymous (attributed to a German monk)

He who drinks well sleeps well. He who sleeps well cannot sin. He who does not sin goes to heaven. Amen.

Anonymous (German saying)

The brewery is the best drug store.

Anonymous

Nor frost, nor snow, nor wind I trow,
Can hurt me if it would,
I am so wrapped within and lapped
With jolly good ale and old.

Anonymous

Bring us in no beef, for there is many bones,
But bring us in good ale, for that go'th down at once.

Anonymous (epitaph in churchyard at Winchester, England, 1764)

Here sleeps in peace a Hampshire grenadier,
Who caught his death by drinking cold small beer;
soldiers, take heed from his untimely fall,
and when you're hot, drink strong, or not at all.

Anonymous

Tons of beef
Oceans of beer
A pretty girl
And a thousand a year!

Anonymous

Landlord, fill the flowing bowl
until it doth run over,
for tonight we'll merry be,
tomorrow we'll be sober.

Anonymous (traditional English carol)

Wassail! wassail! all over the town,
Our bread is white, and our ale it is brown;
Our bowl it is made of the maplin tree,
So here, my good fellow, I'll drink to thee.

The wassailing bowl, with a toast within,
Come fill it up unto the brim;
Come fill it up, so that we may all see;
With the wassailing bowl I'll drink to thee.

Anonymous

Bring us in no brown bread, for that is made of bran,
Nor bring us in no white bread, for therein is no grain;
But bring us in good ale, and bring us in good ale,
For our blessed lady's sake, bring us in good ale.

Anonymous

>Beer! happy produce of our isle,
>Can sinewy strength impart,
>And wearied with fatigue and toil,
>Can cheer each manly heart.

Anonymous

>They talk about their foreign wines—champagne and bright Moselle,
>And think because they're from abroad, that we must like them well,
>And of their wholesome qualities they tell a wondrous tale;
>But sour or sweet, they cannot beat a glass of old English ale.

Anonymous

>I can not eat but little meat,
>   My stomach is not good:
>But sure I think, that I can drink
>   With him that wears a hood.
>Though I go bare, take ye no care,
>   I am nothing acold:
>I stuff my skin, so full within,
>   Of jolly good ale and old,
>Back and side go bare, go bare,
>   Both foot and hand go cold:
>But belly God send thee good ale enough,
>   Whether it be new or old.

Anonymous

>I feel no pain dear mother now
>But Oh, I am so dry!
>O take me to a brewery
>And leave me there to die.

Anonymous

>For it [beer] possesses the essential quality of gulpability. Beer is

more gulpable than any other beverage and consequently it ministers to the desire to drink deeply. When one is really thirsty the nibbling, quibbling, sniffing, squinting technique of the wine connoisseur becomes merely idiotic. Then is the moment of the pint tankard of bitter.

Anonymous

> I desire to end my days in a tavern drinking,
> May some Christian hold for me the glass when I am shrinking;
> That the Cherumbim may cry, when they see me sinking.
> "God be merciful to a soul of this gentleman's way of thinking."

Anonymous ("The Brewer," a song)

> Of all the professions in the town,
> The Brewer's trade hath gain'd renown;
> His liquor reaches up to the crown;
>   Which nobody can deny.
>
> Many new lords from him there did spring,
> Of all the Trades he was still their king;
> For the Brewer had the world in a sling;
>   Which nobody can deny.

Anonymous (a bosun's toast from the Royal Navy)

> Here's to the ships of our navy,
> And the ladies of our land,
> May the first be ever well rigged,
> And the latter ever well manned!

Anonymous (toasts of the world)

Britain	Cheers
France	À votre santé
Germany	Prosit
Greece	Eis hugeian
Israel	L'chayim

Italy	Salute
Japan	Campai
Portugal	A 'voss saudi
Russia	Za vashe zdorovye
Scandinavia	Skoal
Spain	Salud
United States	Bottoms up

Anonymous (a selection of toasts)

Here's to you and you and you!
If I should die and go to heaven, and not find you,
I would turn around and go to hell,
Just to be with you and you and you!

I wish you a Merry Christmas and a happy New Year,
with your pockets full of money, and your cellar full of beer!

Here's to hell! May the stay there
Be as much fun as the way there!

A wee little dog passed a wee little tree.
Said the wee little tree, "Won't you have one on me?"
"No" said the little dog, no bigger than a mouse.
"I just had one—on the house."

Lift 'em high and drain 'em dry
To the guy who says, "My turn to buy!"

Chin chin. (A salutation of English origin from the Edwardian age.)

Here's to you and here's to me,
Here's to the girl with the dimpled knee.
Here's to the boy who fastened the garter;
It wasn't much but a damn good starter.

(Fourteenth century Latin toast)
This is what I now propose:
In a tavern I shall die
With a glass up to my nose
And God's angels standing by
That they may indeed declare
As I take my final tot
May God receive with loving care
Such a decent drunken sot.

May the most you wish for be the least you get.

Anonymous (sixteenth century English proverb)
Wine is but single broth, ale is meat, drink, and cloth.

Saint Arnou (Arnoldus)
From a man's sweat and God's love beer came into the world.

Sir William Ashbless
If but we Christians have our beer, nothing's to fear.

Augsburg, Germany, City Ordinance, thirteenth century
The selling of bad beer is a crime against Christian love.

Hilaire Belloc (1870–1953)
If I ever become a rich man,
    Or if ever I grow to be old,
I will build a house with deep thatch
    To shelter me from the cold,
And there shall the Sussex songs be sung
    And the story of Sussex told.

I will hold my house in the high wood
Within a walk of the sea,
And the men that were boys when I was a boy
Shall sit and drink with me.

From the towns all Inns have been driven: from the villages most . . .
Change your hearts or you will lose your Inns and you will deserve to have
lost them. But when you have lost your Inns drown your empty selves,
for you will have lost the last of England.

Augustine Birrell
All good novels are full of inns. . . . The reason is obvious: the inn is
the finest focal point for the observation of men and manners.

Otto Von Bismarck (1815–1898)
Beer is the cause of all the radical pot-politics that men talk over it.

Humphrey Bogart
The problem with the world is that everybody is three drinks behind.

George Borrow (1803–1881)
Good ale, the true and proper drink of Englishmen. He is not deserving of the name Englishman who speaketh against ale, that is good ale.

Of hard old ale . . . according to my mind, is better than all the wine
in the world.

James Boswell (from *The Life of Samuel Johnson*)
I have heard him assert, that a tavern chair was the throne of human
felicity.

William Bradford (On landing at Plymouth Rock)
For we could not take much time for further search, our victuals
being much spent, especially beer.

Meyer Breslau, 1880

Beer that is not drunk has missed its vocation.

Saint Brigid
(from *The Life of Saint Brigid*)

For when the lepers she nursed implored her for beer and there was none to be had, she changed the water which was used for the bath into an excellent beer, by the sheer strength of her blessing, and dealt it out to the thirsty in plenty.

Tavern scene from Robert Burns's work "Tam O'Shanter" from Geikie's etchings.

Robert Burns

How easy can the barley-bree
Content the quarrel
It's aye the cheapest lawyer's fee
To taste the barrel

Lang may your lum reek [long may your chimney smoke]

Adolphus Busch

It is my aim to win the American people over to our side, to make them all lovers of beer.

You can only drink thirty or forty glasses of beer a day, no matter how rich you are.

Julius Caesar

Beer—a high and mighty liquor.

C. S. Calverley (1831–1884)

O Beer! O Hodgson, Guinness, Allsopp, Bass!
Names that should be on every infant's tongue!

Thomas Campbell

Yes, my soul sentimentally craves British Beer.

Canon of London's St. Paul's Cathedral, eighteenth century

The immense importance of a pint of ale to a common person should never be overlooked.

Dr. S. Carpenter, 1750

A glass of bitter ale or pale ale, taken with the principle meal of the day, does more good and less harm than any medicine the physician can prescribe.

J. Caxton, 1880

Your "wishy washy" wines won't do, and fiery spirits fail,
For nothing blends the heart of friends, like good old English ale.

Miguel Cervantes (from *Don Quixote*)

I drink when I have occasion and sometimes when I have no occasion.

G. K. Chesterton (1874–1936)

And a few men talked of freedom, while England talked of ale.

Before the Roman came to Rye or out to Severn strode,
The rolling English drunkard made the rolling English road.

The righteous minds of innkeepers
    Induce them now and then
To crack a bottle with a friend
    Or treat unmoneyed men.

And I dream of the days when work was scrappy,
And rare in our pockets the mark of the mint,
And we were angry and poor and happy,
And proud of seeing our names in print.

Where you and I went down the lane with ale mugs in our hands.

Winston Churchill
Most people hate the taste of beer—to begin with. It is, however, a prejudice that many have been able to overcome.

John Ciardi
There is nothing wrong with sobriety in moderation.

Fermentation and civilization are inseparable.

John Clare (1793–1864)
Puffing the while his red tipt pipe
He dreams o'er troubles nearly ripe,
Yet, winter's leisure to regale,
Hopes better times, and sips his ale.

I care not with whom I get tipsy
Or where with brown stout I regale,
I'll weather the storm with a gipsy
If he be a lover of ale.

William Combe
Where'er his fancy bids him roam,
In ev'ry Inn he finds a home. . . .
Will not an Inn his cares beguile,
Where on each face he sees a smile?

Richard Corbet (1582–1653)

Mine host was full of beer and history.

Danzig (now Gdansk) City Ordinance, A.D. 1000

Whoever makes poor beer is transferred to the dung-hill.

W. H. Davies (1871–1940), "To Bacchus"

I'm none of those—Oh Bacchus, blush!
    That eat sour pickles with their beer,
To keep their brains and bellies cold;
    Ashamed to let one laughing tear
Escape their hold.

For only just to smell your hops
    Can make me fat and laugh all day,
With appetite for bread and meat:
    I'll not despise bruised apples, they
Make cider sweet.

Tis true I only eat to live,
    But how I live to drink is clear;
A little isle of meat and bread,
    In one vast sea of foaming beer,
And I'm well fed.

Charles Dickens (from *The Pickewick Papers*)

They don't mind it; it's a regular holiday to them—all porter and skittles.

(from *Nicholas Nickelby*)

"Did you ever taste beer?"

"I had a sip of it once," said the small servant.

"Here's a state of things!" cried Mr.Swiveller . . . "She never tasted it—it can't be tasted in a sip!"

John Digby

Tell me where are the beers of yesteryear?
Without beer life appears so austere.

Ecclesiastes 8:15

A man hath no better thing under the sun than to eat and to drink and to be merry.

Egyptian medical book

With beer the spirit is kept in balance with the liver and blood.

Ralph Waldo Emerson (1803–1882)

God made yeast, as well as dough.

Euripides (480–406 B.C.), from *Cyclops*

The man that isn't jolly after drinking,
Is just a drivelling idiot, to my thinking.

Edward Farmer (1809?–1876)

I have no pain, dear mother, now;
But oh! I am so dry:
Just moisten poor Jim's lips once more;
And, mother, do not cry!

George Farquhar (1678–1876)

I have fed purely upon ale; I have eat my ale, drank my ale, and I always sleep upon my ale.

Francis Fawkes (1720–1777), "The Brown Jug," a song

Dear Tom, this brown jug that now foams with mild ale,
(In which I will drink to sweet Nan of the Vale)
Was once Toby Fillpot, a thirsty old soul
As e'er drank a bottle, or fathom'd a bowl;
In bossing about 'twas his praise to excel,
And among jolly topers he bore off the bell.

It chanc'd as in dog-days he sat at his ease
In his flow'r-woven arbour as gay as you please,
With a friend and a pipe puffing sorrows away,
And with honest old stingo was soaking his clay,
His breath-doors of life on a sudden were shut,
And he died full as big as a Dorchester butt.

His body, when long in the ground it had lain,
And time into clay had resolv'd it again,
A potter found out in its covert so snug,
And with part of fat Toby he form'd this brown jug,
Now sacred to friendship, and mirth, and mild ale,
So here's to my lovely sweet Nan of the Vale.

John Fletcher

He who drinks small beer and goes to bed sober,
Falls as the leaves do fall, and dies in rank October;
But he who drinks strong beer and goes to bed mellow,
Lives as he ought to live, and dies an honest fellow.

DRINK to-day and drown all sorrow,
You shall perhaps not do it to-morrow:

Best, while you have it, use your breath;
There'll be no drinking after death.

Sir John Fortescue
They drink no water unless it be . . . for devotion.

Benjamin Franklin
Beer is proof that God loves us.

There are more old drunkards than old doctors.

For there can't be good living where there is not good drinking.

Thomas Fuller, 1732
Everyone hath a penny for the new Alehouse.

John Gay (from, "A Ballad on Ale")
But chief, when to the cheerful glass
From vessel pure they streamlets pass
    The most thy charms prevail;
Then, then, I'll bet, and take the odds,
That nectar, drink of heathen gods,
Was poor, compar'd to Ale.

Give me a bumper, fill it up;
See how it sparkles in the cup;
O how shall I regale!
Can any taste this drink divine
and then compare rum, brandy, wine
or aught with nappy ale?

Gemthorpe, 1790 (in reference to doctors)
To kill us the quicker, you forbid us malt liquor,
Till our bodies consume and our faces grow pale;
But mind it, what pleases, and cures all diseases
Is a comforting dose of good ale!

George Gordon, Lord Byron
What's drinking?
A mere pause from thinking.

W. Scott Griffith
Wine gentrifies, beer unifies.

Thomas Hardy (from *The Mayor of Casterbridge*)
You can have some home-brew, if you want to, you know.

(from *Far From the Madding Crowd*)
Of course you'll have another drop.—of ale—A man's twice the
man afterward. You feel so warm and glorious, . . .

George Herbert
He goes not out of his way that goes to a good inn.

Horace
Now's the time for drinking.

A. E. Housman (1859–1936)
Oh I have been to Ludlow fair
And left my necktie God knows where,
And carried half way home, or near,
Pints and quarts of Ludlow beer:

Say, or what were hop-yards meant,
Or why was Burton built on Trent?
Oh many a peer of England brews
Livelier liquor than the Muse,
And malt does more than Milton can
To justify God's way to man.

Terence, this is stupid stuff:
You eat your victuals fast enough;
There can't be much amiss, 'tis clear,
To see the rate you drink your beer.
But oh, good Lord, the verse you make,
It gives a chap the belly-ache.

The troubles of our proud and angry dust
Are from eternity, and shall not fail
Bear them we can, and if we can we must.
Shoulder the sky, my lad, and drink your ale.

Thomas Hughes (from *Tom Brown's Schooldays*)

Life isn't all beer and skittles; but beer and skittles, or something better of the same sort, must form a good part of every Englishman's education.

Washington Irving

They who drink beer will think beer.

Isaiah 12:3

Let us eat and drink, for tomorrow we shall die.

Samuel Johnson

There is nothing which has yet been contributed by man, by which so much happiness is produced as a good tavern or inn.

Ben Jonson (from *Every Man in his Humour*)

As he brews, so shall he drink.

John Keats

Souls of Poets dead and gone,
What Elysium have ye known,
Happy filed or mossy cavern,
Choicer than the Mermaid Tavern?

Rudyard Kipling

If the home we never write to, and the oaths we never keep,
and all we know most distant and most dear,
Across the snoring barrack-room return to break our sleep,
can you blame us if we soak ourselves in beer?

Pay day came, and with it beer.

That it's beer for the young British soldier—
Beer, beer, beer, for the soldier.

Ere's to English women an' a quart of English beer.

For Maggie has written a letter to give me
my choice between,

The wee little whimpering Love, and the great
    god Nick o' Teen
A million surplus Maggies are willing to bear the
    yoke;
And a woman is only a woman, but a good Cigar
    is a Smoke

Henry Lawson
Beer makes you feel the way you ought to feel without beer.

Tobias Lear
Will you be so good as to desire Mr. Hare to have if he continues to make the best Porter in Philadelphia 3 gross of his best put up for Mt. Vernon? As the President means to visit that place in the recess of Congress and it is probable there will be a large demand for Porter at that time.

H. S. Leigh (1837–1883)
The rapturous, wild and ineffable pleasure
Of drinking at somebody else's expense.

Father LeJuene, 1634
As for drinks, we shall have to make some beer.

Charles G. Leland (1824–1903)
All goned afay mit de lager-beer—
Afay in de ewigkeit!

Henry Wadsworth Longfellow
He who has not been at a tavern knows not what a paradise it is.

(from *Hiawatha*)
What will bring the effervescence,
Who will add the needed factor,
That the beer may foam and sparkle,
May ferment and be delightful?

Walter Map
IF I MUST DIE, let me die drinking in an inn.

Duke of Marlborough
No Soldier can properly fight unless he is properly fed on beef and beer.

Christopher Marlowe
Come my masters, I'll bring you the best beer in Europe.

John Masefield (1878–1967)
Oh some are fond of fiddles, and a song well sung,
And some are all for music for to lilt upon the tongue;
But mouths were made for tankards, and for sucking at the bung,
Says the old bold mate of Henry Morgan.

George Meredith
Ale . . . to Beef what Eve was to Adam.

Henry Miller (1891–1980)
You think a man needs rule, he needs beer.

A. A. Milne (1882–1956)
Of beer an enthusiast has said that it could never be bad, but that some brands might be better than others . . .

John Milton (1608–1674)
Then to the spicy nut brown ale.

Thomas Moore (1779–1852)
If with water you fill up your glasses,
You'll never write anything wise,
For ale is the horse of Parnassus
Which hurries a bard to the skies.

Christopher Morley (1890–1957)
What makes the cider blow its cork
    With such a merry din?
What makes those little bubbles rise
    And dance like harlequin?
It is the fatal apple boys
    The fruit of human sin.

Friedrich Nietzsche (1844–1900)
How much beer is German intelligence.

William Oldys (1606–1671)
Busy, curious, thirsty fly,
Drink with me and drink as I.

George Parsons

It's lonesome away from your kindred and all,
By the campfire light where the wild dingoes call,
But there's nothing so lonesome so morbid or drear
Than to stand in a bar of a Pub With No Beer.

Thomas Peacock (1785–1866)

There are two reasons for drinking: one is when you are thirsty, to cure it; the other, when you are not thirsty, to prevent it. . . . Prevention is better than cure.

The People's Daily, China, 1991

When the beer bubbles, the masses forget their troubles.

Harold Pinter (from *The Caretaker*)

I can't drink Guinness from a thick mug. I only like it out of a thin glass.

Franklin D. Roosevelt, 1933 (on the repeal of Prohibition)

I think this would be a good time for a beer.

Henry Ruggles, 1883

In my innocence I once thought that beer drinking in England was carried to excess, but I was mistaken. Englishmen are in the infant class— in the ABCs—in acquiring a German's education in the practice of drinking beer.

Robert Service

For look! I raise my arm to drink—
A voluntary act, you think
(Nay, Sir, you're grinning).
You're wrong: this stein of beer I've drained
To emptiness was pre-ordained
Since Time's beginning.

William Shakespeare (from *The Merry Wives of Windsor*)

Drink down all unkindness.

(from *A Winter's Tale*)

A quart of ale is a dish fit for a king.

(from *Henry V*)

Would I were in an alehouse in London! I would give all my fame for a pot of ale, and safety.

(from *Othello*)

Cassio: 'Fore God, an excellent song.
Iago: I learned it in England, where indeed they are most potent in potting; your Dane, your German, and your swag-bellied Hollander,—drink, ho!—are nothing to your English.

(from *Othello*)

Most potent in Pottling.

(from *The Taming of the Shrew*)

Were he not warmed with Ale,
This were a bed but cold to sleep soundly.

William Shenstone (1714–1763)

Whoe'er has travell'd life's dull round,
Where'er his stages may have been,
May sigh to think he still has found
The warmest welcome, at an inn.

James Shirley, 1646

I can drink like a fish.

The Reverend Sydney Smith

What two ideas are more in separable than beer and Britannia? What event more awfully important to an English colony than the erection of its first brewhouse?

Sophocles

I recommend bread, meat, vegetables and beer.

James Stephens (1882–1950)

If I asked her master he'd give me a cask a day;

But she, with the beer at hand, not a gill would arrange!

May she marry a ghost and bear him a kitten, and may

The High King of Glory permit her to get the mange.

A cask a day for health!

Jonathan Swift, 1712

We were to do more business after dinner; but after dinner is after dinner—an old saying and a true, much drinking, little thinking.

The Talmud

Up to the age of forty, eating is beneficial; after forty, drinking.

Alfred, Lord Tennyson (1809–1892)

The waiter's hands that reach
To each his perfect pint of stout
His proper chop to each.

William Makepeace Thackeray (1811–1863)

My pulpit is an alehouse bench,
    Whereon I sit so jolly;
A smiling rosy country wench,
    My saint and patron holy.
I kiss her cheek so red and sleek,
    I press her ringlets wavy,
And in her willing ear I speak,
    A most religious Ave.

Dylan Thomas

I think forty-one Guinnesses is piggish.

John Trumbull (1756–1843)

While Briskly to each patriot lip
Walks eager round the inspiring flip;
Delicious draught, whose pow'rs inherit
the quintessence of public spirit.

Thomas Tusser

The hop for his proft I thus do exalt,
It strengtheneth drink, and it flavoreth malt:
And being well brewed, long kept it will last,
and drawing abide—if you draw not too fast.

Mark Twain

Every man that had any respect for himself would have got drunk, as was the custom of the country on all occasions of public moment.

United States Department of Agriculture, 1866

. . . a moderate use of beer will aid digestion, quicken the powers of life, and give elasticity to the body and mind.

Louis Untermeyer (1885–1977)

Life, alas,
Is very drear.
Up with the glass!
Down with the beer!

Tom Waits

I don't have a drink problem except when I can't get one.

George Washington (on the Constitutional Convention)

The business being closed, the members adjourned to the City Tavern.

Evelyn Waugh

Beer is acceptable very late at night at the end of a party.—It is a fine honest staple rather than a theme for poetry.

Mr. Weir, 1800

In London it is our beer that stands foremost in the ranks of pleasant thoughts . . . Therefore it is that the cry of "beer" falls like music on the ear.

Oscar Wilde

Work is the curse of the drinking classes.

Harry Leon Wilson

While beer brings gladness, don't forget that water only makes you wet.

Thomas Wilson (from *The Rule of Reason*, 1551)

He that drinks well, sleeps well.

John Woodforde (from *Diary of a Country Parson*, April 15, 1778)

Brewed a vessel of strong Beer today. My two large Piggs . . . got so amazingly drunk by it, that they were not able to stand and appeared like dead things almost, and so remained all night from dinner-time today. I never say Piggs so drunk in my life.

Xenophon

For drink there was beer which was very strong when not mingled with water, but was agreeable to those who were used to it. They drank this with a reed, out of the vessel that held the beer, upon which they saw the barley swim.

Frank Zappa

For any country to be a country, you have to have an air force, a football team, and a beer. You can get by without the air force and the football team, but you have to have a beer.

A Winter Warmer (G. Smith), 1993

One dismal night in a nameless bar,
while solving problems of the world
we may have gone just one too far.
And, caressing pints with fingers curled,
thought better of going out.

No chasing of the here-say brews
through countless tap rooms of the town,
we stayed upon our barstool pews;
and collecting coin for one last round,
ordered a final stout.

The snow outside had changed to sleet;
we nursed the draught along t'ward morn,
and listening to the weather beat,
dismissed all motions to adjourn
by ordering up two more.

We'd later wonder what was said,
and from where we got such sodden bills.
Profound ideas all had fled,
cause surely we had had our fill.
But you bought just one more.

Some poor folks will never know,
the warmth within the tavern room
while fending off a driven storm,
sweet solace from the winter's gloom
and comfort for the soul.

And who could ever ask for more;
than one last beer before the door.

Bibliography

Abel, Bob. *The Beer Book*. London: Music Sales Limited, 1981.

Ade, George. *The Old-Time Saloon*. New York: Old Town Books, 1993.

Anderson, Will. *The Beer Book*. Princeton, N.J.: The Pyne Press, 1973.

——. *From Beer to Eternity*. Lexington, Mass.: The Stephen Greene Press, 1987.

Barnard, Alfred. *Bass & Co. Limited*. Burton-on-Trent, England: N.p., 1889.

Baron, Stanley. *Brewed in America: A History of Beer and Ale in the United States*. Boston: Little, Brown, 1962.

Barrows, Susanna, and Robin Room. *Drinking, Behavior and Belief in Modern History*. Berkeley: University of California Press, n.d.

Batterberry, Michael and Ariane. *On The Town in Old New York*. New York: Charles Scribner's Sons, 1973.

Bayles, W. Harrison. *Old Taverns of New York*. New York: Frank Allaben Genealogical Co., 1915.

Bickerdyke, John. *The Curiosities of Ale & Beer*. 1889. Reprint, London: Spring Books Westbook House, 1965.

Bowen, Catherine Drinker. *Miracle at Philadelphia*. New York: Book of the Month Club, 1986.

Brown, John Hull. *Early American Beverages*. New York: Bonanza Books, 1966.

Butcher, Alan D. *Ale & Beer: A Curious History*. Toronto: McClelland & Stewart Inc., 1989.

Clark, Peter. *The English Alehouse: A Social History 1200–1830*. New York: Longman, n.d.

Dallas, John, and Charles McMaster. *The Beer Drinkers Companion*. Edinburgh, Scotland: The Edinburgh Publishing Company, 1993.

Daniels, Ray. *Designing Great Beers*. Boulder, Colo.: Brewers Publications, 1997.

Digby, Joan, and John Digby. *Inspired by Drink*. New York: Morrow, 1988.

Downard, William L. *Dictionary of the History of the American Brewing and Distilling Industries*. Westport, Conn.: Greenwood Press, 1980.

Doxat, John. *The Book of Drinking*. London: Triune Books, 1973.

Earle, Alice Morse. *Stage Coach and Tavern Days*. New York: MacMillan, 1900.

———. *Customs and Fashions in Old New England*. Williamstown, Mass.: Corner House Publishers, 1983.

Erikson, Jack. *Star Spangled Beer*. Reston, Va.: RedBrick Press, 1987.

———. *Brewed in California*. Reston, Va.: RedBrick Press, 1993.

"Everything You Always Wanted to Know About Beer." *Zymurgy,* Summer 1993.

Farb, Peter, and George Armelagos. *Consuming Passions: The Anthropology of Eating*. Boston: Houghton Mifflin, 1980.

Fennelly, Catherine. *Life in an Old New England Village*. New York: Crowell, 1969.

Fix, George, and Laurie Fix. *Oktoberfest, Vienna, Märzen*. Boulder, Colo.: Brewers Publications, 1991.

Fleming, Alice. *Alcohol the Delightful Poison*. New York: Delacorte Press, n.d.

Forget, Carl. *Dictionary of Beer and Brewing*. Boulder, Colo.: Brewers Publications, 1988.

Foster, Terry. *Pale Ale*. Boulder, Colo.: Brewers Publications, 1990.

———. *Porter*. Boulder, Colo.: Brewers Publications, 1992.

Gayre, G. R. *Wassail in Mazers of Mead*. London: Phillimore & Co., 1948.

Gies, Joseph, and Frances Gies. *Cathedral, Forge, and Waterwheel Technology and Invention in the Middle Ages*. New York: HarperCollins, 1994.

Grossman, Harold J. *Grossman's Guide to Wines, Spirits, and Beers*. New York: Charles Scribner's Sons, 1955.

Grun, Bernard. *The Timetables of History*. New York: Simon & Schuster, 1975.

Guinard, Jean-Xavier. *Lambic*. Boulder, Colo.: Brewers Publications, 1990.

Haiber, William Paul, and Robert Haiber. *A Short, but Foamy, History of Beer*. La Grangeville, N.Y.: Info Devel Press, 1993.

Jackson, Michael. *The New World Guide to Beer*. Philadelphia: Running Press, 1988.

———. *The Pocket Guide to Beer*. New York: Simon and Schuster, 1991.

———. *Jackson's Beer Companion*. Philadelphia: Running Press, 1993.

Johnson, Steve. *America's Best Brews*. Houston: Gulf Publishing Co., 1997.

Lathrop, Elise. *Early American Inns and Taverns*. New York: Arno Press, 1977.

Lender, Mary Edward, and James Kirby Martin. *Drinking in America: A History*. New York: The Free Press, 1982.

Lewis, Michael J. *Stout*. Boulder, Colo.: Brewers Publications, 1995.

Marchant, W. T. *In Praise of Ale*. London: George Redway, 1888.

McNulty, Henry. *Drinking in Vogue*. New York: The Vendome Press, 1978.

Meier, Gary, and Gloria Meier. *Brewed in the Pacific Northwest*. Seattle: Fjord Press, 1991.

Mendel, Jeff. *Brewers Resources Directory 1990–1991*. Boulder, Colo.: Brewers Publications, 1990.

Mendelsohn, Oscar. *The Dictionary of Drink and Drinking*. New York: Hawthorn Books Inc., 1965.

Miller, Dave. *Continental Pilsener*. Boulder, Colo.: Brewers Publications, 1989.

———. *Brewing the World's Great Beers*. Pownal, Vt.: Storey, 1992.

Morini, John. *America Eats Out*. New York: Morrow, 1991.

Noonan, Gregory J. *Scotch Ale*. Boulder, Colo.: Brewers Publications, 1993.

Prial, Frank J. "The Man Who Rescued a Brewery." *New York Times,* July 11, 1984.

Protz, Roger. *The European Beer Almanac*. Moffat, Scotland: Lochar Publishing, 1991.

———. *The Real Ale Drinker's Almanac*. Moffat, Scotland: Lochar Publishing, 1991.

———. *The Ale Trail*. London: Eric Dobby Publishing Ltd., 1995.

———. *Classic Stout & Porter*. London: Prion Books, 1997.

Rae, Simon, ed. *The Faber Book of Drink, Drinkers, and Drinking*. London: Faber & Faber Limited, 1991.

Rajotte, Pierre. *Belgian Ale*. Boulder, Colo.: Brewers Publications, 1992.

Randel, William Pierce. *Centennial: American Life in 1876*. New York: Chilton, 1969.

Rhodes, Christine. *The Encyclopedia of Beer*. Henry Holt and Company, 1995.

Rice, Kym S. *Early American Taverns: For the Entertainment of Friends and Strangers*. Chicago: Regnery Gateway, 1983.

Robertson, James D. *The Great American Beer Book*. New York: Warner Books, 1978.

———. *The Beer-Tasters Log*. Pownal, Vt.: Storey, 1996.

St. James Gate Brewery. Dublin: Arthur Guinness, Son & Co., 1931.

Schulter, Herman. *Brewery Workers Movement in America*. Cincinnati: IUUBWA, 1910.

Smith, Gregg. "Beer in the Civil War." *All About Beer Magazine,* April/May 1993.

———. "Upstate New York, Regional Breweries." *BarleyCorn,* July/August 1993.

———. *The Beer Enthusiast's Guide*. Pownal, Vt.: Storey, 1994.

———. *Beer: A History*. New York: Avon, 1995.

Smith, Page. *A New Age Now Begins*. New York: McGraw-Hill, 1976.

Snyder, Stephen. *The Brew Master's Bible*. New York: HarperCollins, 1997.

Tunis, Edward. *Colonial Living*. Toronto: Fitz Henry & Whiteside Limited, 1957.

———. *Frontier Living*. New York: Crowell, 1961.

Van Wieren, Dale P. *American Breweries II*. West Point, Pa.: Eastern Coast Breweriana Association, 1995.

Wagner, Rich. "Brewing in the 17th Century." *Zymurgy,* Spring 1992.

Warner, Eric. *German Wheat Beer*. Boulder, Colo.: Brewers Publications, 1992.

Weiner, Michael A. *The Taster's Guide to Beer*. New York: Collier Books, 1977.

Wheeler, Graham, and Roger Protz. *Brew Your Own Real Ale at Home*. St. Albans, England: 1993.

Wilford, John Noble. "Trade or Colonialism? Ruins May Give Answer." *New York Times,* May 25, 1993.

100 Years of Brewing. Supplement to the *Western Brewer*. New York & Chicago: H. S. Rich & Co., 1903.

About the Authors

Gregg Smith is an award-winning author and speaker on beer and brewing. He has been a featured lecturer at the Smithsonian Institution and the prestigious Culinary Institute of America. Frequently appearing as a beer expert on national and international radio and television, he is a sought-after speaker who has hosted beer dinners at fine restaurants across the United States. His other speaking engagements include the Great American Beer Festival, historical societies, Beer Camp, and beer appreciation clubs around the country.

He has served as cochair of the North American Guild of Beer Writers and as both a member of the board and associate director of the Beer Judge Certification Program. He holds the rank of National Beer Judge and has judged four consecutive years at the Great American Beer Festival.

Gregg is managing editor of the *Beer & Tavern Chronicle*, a national monthly beer periodical, field editor of the *Brew Review*, and guest editor in *Yankee Brew News*. His many articles have also appeared in numerous publications throughout the United States.

Writing awards Gregg has won in 1997 from the North American Guild of Beer Writers include two gold Quill and Tankards for editorials and humor, and two bronze Quill and Tankards for columns and humor/fiction. He was also named 1997 Beer Writer of the Year. In 1996, Gregg received a gold Quill and Tankard for history writing; a silver Quill and Tankard for a book; two bronze Quill and Tankards for travel and brewing; and an honorable mention Quill and Tankard for columns. He was also named Beer Writer of the Year—First Runner Up in 1996.

Carrie Getty is an avid beer researcher with substantial experience in beer judging and evaluation. Ms. Getty has been a speaker at various beer clubs around the country and at Beer Camp in Fort Mitchell, Kentucky, and the Oldenberg Brewery.

Carrie holds the rank of National Beer Judge and serves as an official exam administrator for the Beer Judge Certification Program. She has taught beer judging and evaluation classes. She travels extensively throughout the United States and Europe with her husband, Gregg Smith, researching breweries and the world's beer styles.

An award-winning homebrewer, Carrie was a past vice president of the New York City Homebrewers Guild, and founder and past president of the High Desert Brewers Association.

Carrie is the associate editor of the *Beer & Tavern Chronicle*. She also antagonizes the organizing committee of the Mountain Brewers Beer Festival, an event that attracts over three hundred beers from North America and Europe to an annual festival held on the first Saturday of June in Idaho Falls, Idaho.

Index

Index